A Wayfarer's Guide to Bringing the Sacred Home

A Wayfarer's Guide to Bringing the Sacred Home

by Joseph Sheppherd

Bahá'í
PUBLISHING
Wilmette, Illinois

Bahá'í Publishing
Wilmette, Illinois 60091-2886
Copyright © 2002 by the National Spiritual Assembly of the Bahá'ís
of the United States
All rights reserved. Published 2002
Printed in the United States of America
on acid-free paper ∞

05   04   03   02   4   3   2   1

Library of Congress Cataloging-in-Publication Data
Sheppherd, Joseph.
    A wayfarer's guide to bringing the sacred home / by Joseph
Sheppherd.
        p. cm.
    Includes bibliographical references (p.) and index.
    ISBN 1-931847-02-9 (alk. paper)
    1. Spiritual life—Bahai Faith. 2. Bahai Faith—Doctrines. I.
Title.

BP380 .S54 2002
297.9'344—dc21
                                            2001043338

Design by Suni D. Hannan

There is nothing greater or more blessed than the Love of God! It gives healing to the sick, balm to the wounded, joy and consolation to the whole world, and through it alone can man attain Life Everlasting. The *essence* of all religions is the Love of God, and it is the foundation of all the sacred teachings.

—Bahá'í scripture

The whole earth is one home, and all peoples, did they but know it, are bathed in the oneness of God's mercy.

—Bahá'í scripture

Contents

A Wayfarer's Guide to Bringing the Sacred Home

Introduction

Each of us brings a variety of things home in the course of our lifetime, both into the place where we dwell and into the home within our heart. Every day we make choices and encounter situations that have lasting effects on our lives, our relationships, and our view of the world. Some of what we bring home and end up carrying in our hearts brings us joy, and some is painful. Fortunately, as time goes on, we learn to be more selective and deliberate in choosing what we bring into our lives. We discover that some things are more meaningful and spiritually satisfying than others. For many of us this is the beginning of a lifelong process of personal transformation. We come to see things around us in a new light and seek the divine purpose in the world, and we begin to bring this sacredness home.

A Wayfarer's Guide to Bringing the Sacred Home is a journey through three important relationships: the connection we have with our own inner being, the bond we develop with the members of our family, and the contribution we make to our community. This book endeavors to guide the wayfarer in discovering the sacredness to be found within each of these relationships. Each chapter touches upon important issues within the greater themes of self, family, and community. Extracts from Bahá'í scripture are interspersed throughout each chapter, providing material for meditation and reflection.

Together we will explore some of the spiritual features of the self, that part of us which forms our inner being. We will find that by bringing our Creator home into our lives and utilizing the power of prayer, we acquire the means to grow spiritually and deal with life's tests. We will examine several of the dynamics of the family unit and its component relationships. We will discover that by endeavoring to build family unity and establish marital harmony, we can raise our children to be bright emblems of the future. We will look beyond the home to the common experience we share with the rest of the world community. We will find that expanding our circle of unity requires that we begin to appreciate and find common ground with others whom we see as different from ourselves. By looking within ourselves and identifying the prejudices we must overcome, we can begin working toward racial understanding and harmony between the genders. We will find ways of celebrating diversity, serving the needs of our community, and helping to bring the peoples of the world together as one human family.

A Wayfarer's Guide to Bringing the Sacred Home offers a Bahá'í perspective on the inherent receptiveness of our inner being to the sacred Word of God. It suggests ways to achieve a profound sense of reverence within the family and to appreciate the diversity of the people of this planet. This perspective centers on the concepts of unity and oneness, which are central to the teachings of the Bahá'í Faith. The source of these concepts is Bahá'u'lláh (1817–92), the founder of the Bahá'í Faith. They are the central themes woven throughout the more than one hundred volumes of scripture that Bahá'u'lláh wrote during his forty-year ministry. Because he was persecuted by the Persian and Ottoman Empires, Bahá'u'lláh was a prisoner and an exile from the age of thirty-three until his death. Though he wrote in Persian and Arabic, a substantial number of his works have been translated into English and many other languages.

A Wayfarer's Guide to Bringing the Sacred Home incorporates passages from a number of Bahá'u'lláh's works as well as from the writings of three other figures who are important in the history and teachings of the Bahá'í Faith: the Báb (1819–50), who was the forerunner of Bahá'u'lláh and was, Bahá'ís believe, a Prophet of God in his own right; 'Abdu'l-Bahá (1844–1921), who was Bahá'u'lláh's eldest son and the appointed interpreter of Bahá'u'lláh's writings and teachings; and Shoghi Effendi (1897–1957), who was the great-grandson of Bahá'u'lláh and the head of the Bahá'í Faith after 'Abdu'l-Bahá's death in 1921.

Throughout his works Bahá'u'lláh draws attention to the need for unity in the world and to three essential Bahá'í beliefs. First, he reminds us that there is only one God. Regardless of the variety of names by which we refer to Him—names such as *God, Dios, Allah,* or *Yahweh*—all refer to the same Divine Being. Second, Bahá'u'lláh teaches that there is only one humanity, one human race. God is the creator of all, and no group or nation can lay exclusive claim to His love or grace. In the sight of God there are no racial, national, or economic distinctions, for no particular group of people is inherently superior to another. Third, he teaches that there is only one religion—the religion of God. God sends Prophets to humanity from time to time, and all progressively develop the same religion of God, even though it comes to different people under different names. Bahá'u'lláh teaches that the age in which we live is the age of the maturation of humankind, a time when humanity is destined to come together as one family and regard each other as fellow believers in one God.

A Wayfarer's Guide to Bringing the Sacred Home looks at the personal, social, and cultural benefits of unity, its timeliness today, and the means for its achievement. Over the past century or so since the passing of Bahá'u'lláh in 1892, the word *unity* has gained several new meanings and connotations. For this reason it will be helpful to clarify what it means here. In its vernacular usage, unity is often tacitly defined as some movement toward sameness. This is not what Bahá'ís believe unity to be. Unity is not uniformity; it is the organic cohesion of varying elements which, Bahá'u'lláh teaches, must embrace and accommodate diversity:

> Consider the flowers of a garden. Though differing in kind, color, form and shape, yet, inasmuch as they are refreshed by the waters of one spring, revived by the breath of one wind, invigorated by the rays of one sun, this diversity increaseth their charm and addeth unto their beauty. How unpleasing to the eye if all the flowers and plants, the leaves and blossoms, the fruit, the branches and the trees of that garden were all of the same shape and color! Diversity of hues, form and shape enricheth and adorneth the garden, and heighteneth the effect thereof.[1]

At the close of the nineteenth century, Bahá'u'lláh identified the achievement of unity in diversity as our greatest social need. This is still true at the dawn of the third millennium. Indeed Bahá'u'lláh's life and teachings serve as a testimony to the pressing needs of this day and age. We are fortunate that there were contemporary historians who witnessed and wrote about the unparalleled events of Bahá'u'lláh's life and ministry; however, they were often at a loss for words in their attempts to describe him. Perhaps the best attempt occurred just two years before his passing, when Bahá'u'lláh himself welcomed one of the few Westerners ever to meet him. The visitor was Edward Granville Browne, a rising young orientalist and future professor of Cambridge University. In the words of Professor Browne:

> The face of him on whom I gazed I can never forget, though I cannot describe it. Those piercing eyes seemed to read one's very soul; power and authority sat on that ample brow. . . . No need to ask in whose presence I stood, as I bowed myself before one who is the object of a devotion and love which kings might envy and emperors sigh for in vain![2]

In his memoirs Professor Browne recounts that Bahá'u'lláh, in a mild, dignified voice, invited him to be seated and spoke to him:

> Praise be to God that thou hast attained! . . . Thou hast come to see a prisoner and an exile. . . . We desire but the good of the world and the happiness of the nations; yet they deem us a stirrer up of strife and sedition worthy of bondage and banishment. . . . That all nations should become one in faith and all men as brothers; that the bonds of affection and unity between the sons of men should be strengthened; that diversity of religion should cease, and differences of race

be annulled—what harm is there in this? . . .
Yet so it shall be; these fruitless strifes, these
ruinous wars shall pass away, and the "Most
Great Peace" shall come. . . . Do not you in
Europe need this also? Is not this that which
Christ foretold? . . . Yet do we see your kings
and rulers lavishing their treasures more
freely on means for the destruction of the
human race than on that which would con-
duce to the happiness of mankind. . . . These
strifes and this bloodshed and discord must
cease, and all men be as one kindred and
one family. . . .[3]

Each Prophet of God is a wondrous Teacher
sent to help humanity advance to the next stage
in its spiritual education; the Prophets' abilities are beyond our understanding. In a sense,
attempting to characterize the Prophets of God
is like trying to describe the sun. Though its
light and warmth can be described, in the end,
words fail to convey its complete reality.

The analogy of a mirror and its relationship
to the sun is helpful in portraying the role of
the Prophets of God. Like a perfect mirror placed
in the sunlight, Bahá'u'lláh and all of the other
Prophets of God reflect the glory of God. Bahá'u'lláh and these Prophets are not God Himself, just as the reflection in the mirror is not
the sun. Although the bright reflection and the
sun itself appear equal, and both shed their

light and warmth upon us, they are separate. It is impossible for us to approach the sun without being consumed in a mighty force beyond our comprehension, but we can draw near to the reflection in the mirror and understand something of the sun's light and power. Similarly the Prophets serve as intermediaries between God and humanity, for they are the mirror in whose reflection we can see the attributes of God.

There have been many Prophets of God, and there will be more in the future. We know this is true because God has promised never to abandon us. The names of some of the Prophets He has sent may be familiar to us: Abraham, Krishna, Moses, Zoroaster, Buddha, Christ, Muḥammad, the Báb, and most recently Bahá'-u'lláh. We can be sure that there were others whose lives and teachings are not known to us because they appeared before the advent of written communication. One after the other their revelations have been progressive, each building on what has come before and focusing on the next stage in humanity's individual and collective spiritual development. In this age the focus is unity.

May this book serve as a guide on your sacred journey to find a spiritual "home." Whether you seek a spiritual perspective on personal transformation, on the health of your family, or on the well-being of your community, the inspirational Bahá'í scripture included in *A Wayfarer's Guide to Bringing the Sacred Home* can help you in the journey toward greater spiritual understanding. Spiritual growth is not a sudden occurrence or a one-shot deal; it is a gradual process that starts with a leap of faith and grows through consistent efforts to draw closer to God. May His Word be a source of inspiration to you in everything you do, from the most simple and ordinary of acts to the most noble and courageous. There is no great secret to the journey. All it requires is the willingness to turn toward Him and a sincere desire to embrace that which will bring Him into your heart, your home, and your community.

Part 1

Turning to God

*Beware lest the transitory things of human life withhold
you from turning unto God, the True One.*
—BAHÁ'U'LLÁH

*O thou who art turning thy face towards God!
Close thine eyes to all things else, and open them to
the realm of the All-Glorious. Ask whatsoever
thou wishest of Him alone; seek whatsoever
thou seekest from Him alone.*
—'ABDU'L-BAHÁ

The first step on the path toward spirituality is to turn in the direction of that which we seek. This is only logical. Knowing which way to turn, however, is not always easy. The world is filled with material pursuits, and clear evidences of spirituality within it are often hard to find. In spite of this, each of us in our own way eventually encounters traces of our Creator. If we look carefully enough we discover that the traces are hidden in plain sight and manifest in everything around us. Even before we begin to recognize them consciously, our soul may begin to respond to these traces. As a creation of God, every soul has the innate desire and ability to seek and to know its Creator. However, to turn toward God and journey along the path that draws us closer to Him is a conscious choice and a continuous act of volition.

Once we begin to turn toward God and embark upon our journey, the world becomes a different place. Everything is made new before our eyes. We begin to understand that we have been born into this world for a reason, that our life has meaning and purpose. This is the starting point on a journey that will lead us through many spiritually beneficial conditions and experiences. The world is vast enough and large enough for each of us to take a different path, yet by various routes we can all draw closer to God.

Eventually the path will go beyond this life, yet the spiritual journey will continue. In the meantime there is much to learn. Here, in the material world, we must learn to tread the spiritual path with practical feet. Like those who carry water from a stream in jars on their heads, we must learn to conduct our lives while balancing that which is most precious to us. Learning to balance the spiritual and material aspects of life is an ongoing process. We must turn to God in our daily lives, not only when all else has failed us, but also when things are running smoothly.

We should strive not to be distracted by either the difficulty or the ease we encounter in life, for one follows on the heels of the other, and both have profound lessons to offer. Everything in this world is brief, and the earth is our home only for a short time. We move on, and the world stays behind. But in the brief span of time we are here, there is much to be learned. Chapters 1 through 4 consider the importance of bringing God into our lives through the use of prayer and how to grow spiritually while successfully coping with life's challenges.

1

Bringing God into Our Lives

Let the flame of the love of God burn brightly within your radiant hearts.
— BAHÁ'U'LLÁH

Each of us has different experiences in life, different thoughts and understandings. Even when we are looking at the same objects, we don't necessarily see them in the same way. Our views of the world are as unique as we are. When we look up at the night sky, we all see stars, but our perceptions of what we see may be very different. Some of us perceive patterns and connect the points of light into constellations; others see the interstices, the dark spaces between the stars. Some see the stars in two dimensions, arrayed like electric lights of various sizes on the ceiling; others perceive a third dimension of depth in their varying magnitudes. To some the sun and the stars are different; to others they are the same thing, with the one simply being closer to us than the rest. When we represent stars graphically, some draw them scintillating with five, six, or more points; others just make dots. Regardless of how we see or portray them, stars are what they are, and their reality does not change. Only our perceptions of them differ.

The same is true of our individual understandings of God. We all have varying concepts of God because we have different experiences in life, different thoughts and perceptions. If we have different ways of seeing things such as stars, then it is natural to have different ways of conceptualizing something that cannot be seen, like God. Of course, whatever concept we create can never portray God sufficiently. Regardless of what we believe about God, His reality is not altered. God is what God is. Yet our concepts of God are bound to change and develop as we grow spiritually. As we advance in our spiritual understandings, our concepts will move away from simplistic definitions and will more appropriately reflect the reality that is ever unfolding before us.

Examples of concepts that change as we gain greater insight into them are numerous. For instance, the words *up* and *down* are among the first we learn as children. They represent simple concepts, and their meanings change little as we grow older. As children, if we were asked to explain up and down we might simply point above our heads and below our feet; and as adults we might define them as opposite orientations along a vertical axis. Both explanations are determined by our relative age and experience, and both are basically very similar. No matter how old we may be, we find up and down easy to explain because they are simple and straightforward concepts.

The concepts of up and down become less simple, however, if we move away from the surface of the earth. If we were to be suspended one inch off the ground, up and down would still have meaning, and at one foot it would be pretty much the same. Even at an altitude of one mile we would still retain a sense of up and down, and we would have to turn completely around to see the entire horizon. But at one hundred miles above the earth the horizon would no longer be flat; it would curve into a long arc. And at one thousand miles we would be able to see the entire circle of the globe. At one million miles the circle would have greatly diminished and the earth would be a mere dot of light. At a distance of one billion miles it would be difficult to locate our home planet, and at one trillion miles the earth would be completely invisible against the stars of the Milky Way.

Out in interstellar space we would notice that there is no "up" or "down" as we know it. These terms would lose their meaning. Looking out on the universe, we would have to find a new way to explain our orientation. In the light of this new situation we might try to determine precisely at what distance from earth the concepts of up and down lose their meaning. Eventually we would discover that it isn't the concepts that change, but rather our understanding of the limitations inherent within them that does. These limitations are always there; we just can't see them from our vantage point on earth. They can only truly be understood in retrospect.

Up and down are neither right nor wrong, true nor untrue; they are earthbound concepts that are useful and appropriate in this physical world, and they are adequate for as long as we are on it. This is true of many other concepts and serves as a good analogy for our understanding of spiritual matters. Because we have been born into this physical existence on earth, it is reasonable to look at religion and come to the conclusion that humans are physical beings in search of spirituality. However, as reasonable as this assumption may be, it is based on a very limited understanding of who and what we human beings really are. When we are caught up in the daily practical concerns of our physical existence, it is difficult to discover that we are spiritual beings in the midst of the physical experience of life. This is one of the reasons why God has sent us Prophets such as Moses, Christ, Muḥammad, the Báb, and most recently Bahá'-u'lláh. They remind us that we are essentially spiritual beings who are on this earth for a reason and that we are here only for a short time. They tell us that we will move beyond this physical plane of existence to a spiritual condition that cannot be adequately described in words. They teach us that where we are going is wondrous beyond our imagination and that there are certain things we need to understand before we go on to the life hereafter.

He, verily, will aid everyone that aideth Him, and will remember everyone that remembereth Him.[1]

Put thy whole confidence in the grace of God, thy Lord. Let Him be thy trust in whatever thou doest, and be of them that have submitted themselves to His Will. Let Him be thy helper and enrich thyself with His trea-

sures, for with Him are the treasuries of the heavens and of the earth.[2]

Our concepts of God are limited by our experiences here on earth. Depending on what language we speak, our particular word for God is likely to have associations with root words such as *strong, great, lofty, shining,* or *spirit.* To some degree we have to anthropomorphize God—that is, to refer to God with the pronoun *He* and visualize Him as human—to begin to understand Him. We are told in the sacred scriptures of most religions that we were created in God's image. Perhaps we look at ourselves in a mirror and then imagine what God might look like. But we are asked to look deeper. We may look within ourselves and find a capacity for caring and love, or perhaps as we experience the unconditional love and compassion of a parent or other loved one, we begin to understand that God is the source of compassion and loving-kindness, that God is love. The sacred scriptures of nearly every religion refer to God as omnipotent, omniscient, and omnipresent, as being all-powerful, all-knowing, and everywhere at the same time. Understanding what these concepts mean is more difficult than simply looking in a mirror, because there is no one on earth who has these qualities. These concepts are more difficult to grasp because they are abstractions; to better understand them we need to relate them to things within our own experience through the use of analogy.

O thou who art turning thy face towards God! Close thine eyes to all things else, and open them to the realm of the All-Glorious. Ask whatsoever thou wishest of Him alone; seek whatsoever thou seekest from Him alone. With a look He granteth a hundred thousand hopes, with a glance He healeth a hundred thousand incurable ills, with a nod He layeth balm on every wound, with a glimpse He freeth the hearts from the shackles of grief. He doeth as He doeth, and what recourse have we? He carrieth out His Will, He ordaineth what He pleaseth. Then better for thee to bow down thy head in submission, and put thy trust in the All-Merciful Lord.[3]

Pray to and seek assistance from God, and ... supplicate and implore His aid.[4]

When one supplicates to his Lord, turns to Him and seeks bounty from His Ocean, this supplication brings light to his heart, illumination to his sight, life to his soul and exaltation to his being.[5]

Although describing an abstraction by analogy has its limitations, parables and allegories, similes and metaphors are our only means of understanding abstract things that are beyond our realm of experience. For example, God is often described as a father figure. This is easily understood by people who belong to a social structure that is based upon patriarchy. It is something familiar to us. Yet we can also see beyond this kind of analogy and realize that God is neither male nor female, and we can at least begin to imagine God without gender. As we mature, we learn to see the inherent limitations of our previous understandings. When we were children and heard that God has the whole world in His hands, it was reasonable for us to assume that God was big, very big. Later, when we learned the difference between figurative analogies and the literal meanings of words, we came to understand that God is neither big nor little, that God has no size.

Male and *female, big* and *little* are like the concepts of up and down. They only apply to the physical universe. The reality of God is infinitely greater than these. Analogies do, however, serve a purpose. They are the starting points of understanding. Here in the physical world, we begin a process of learning that will last as long as the soul endures, through all of eternity.

Nearness to God is possible through devotion to Him, through entrance into the Kingdom and service to humanity; it is attained by unity with mankind and through loving-kindness to all; it is dependent upon investigation of truth, acquisition of praiseworthy virtues, service in the cause of universal peace and personal sanctification. In a word, nearness to God necessitates sacrifice of self, severance and the giving up of all to Him. Nearness is likeness.[6]

Remembrance of God is like the rain and dew which bestow freshness and grace on flowers and hyacinths, revive them and cause them to acquire fragrance, redolence and renewed charm. . . . Strive thou, then, to praise and glorify God by night and by day, that thou mayest attain infinite freshness and beauty.[7]

———————————

Bahá'u'lláh tells us that God is ultimately unknowable, that we can never fully comprehend our Creator. God cannot be defined by anyone but God. We can know something of His creation, but no matter how much we understand, God is still infinitely greater than the thoughts of the whole of creation. This is an important lesson in humility for us. As witnessed everywhere in nature, lesser things can never understand greater things. Rocks can't comprehend the nature of plants, plants can't comprehend the nature of animals, animals can't comprehend the nature of humans, and humans can't comprehend the nature of God. But still we are placed on earth for a purpose, and we have always needed ways to contemplate our Creator. The Prophets of God teach us about the qualities, or attributes, of God, enabling us to transcend some of the limitations of definitions and analogies.

Rely upon God. Trust in Him. Praise Him, and call Him continually to mind. He verily turneth trouble into ease, and sorrow into solace, and toil into utter peace. He verily hath dominion over all things.[8]

When a man turns his face to God he finds sunshine everywhere.[9]

The knowledge of God is beyond all knowledge, and it is the greatest glory of the human world.[10]

The attributes of God are qualities that draw our attention to aspects of His interaction with us and all of creation. They are the traces of the essence of our Creator. These divine attributes appear within the prayers and sacred writings of all religions in various forms, where God is referred to as the Almighty, the Powerful, the Helper, the All-Merciful, the Bestower, the All-Bountiful, the All-Knowing, the All-Wise, the Forgiving, the Compassionate. Contemplating these attributes one by one allows us to focus on a particular characteristic of our Creator and look deep within ourselves. We can examine our own sense of inner strength, helpfulness, mercy, generosity, bounty, knowledge, wisdom, forgiveness, and compassion. These are potential qualities within all of us that reflect the attributes of God. They are, as Bahá'u'lláh explains, God's image within us:

> To give and to be generous are attributes of Mine; well is it with him that adorneth himself with My virtues.[11]

All together these qualities form the virtues we are told to incorporate into our lives. We are familiar with many of these virtues: kindness, excellence, faithfulness, generosity, honesty, justice, love, reverence, and unity, to name only a few. These are qualities that the Prophets of God have told us to strive to cultivate because they aid our individual spiritual development. These virtues are also the firm ground on which successful families are built, and ultimately they form the moral foundations of society.

The soul does not evolve from degree to degree as a law—it only evolves nearer to God, by the Mercy and Bounty of God.[12]

All is in the hands of God, and without Him there can be no health in us![13]

In truth, the fruit of human existence is the love of God, for this love is the spirit of life, and the eternal bounty.[14]

Selected Prayers from Bahá'í Scripture

Praised be Thou, O Lord my God! Every time I attempt to make mention of Thee, I am hindered by the sublimity of Thy station and the over-powering greatness of Thy might. For were I to praise Thee throughout the length of Thy dominion and the duration of Thy sovereignty, I would find that my praise of Thee can befit only such as are like unto me, who are themselves Thy creatures, and who have been generated through the power of Thy decree and been fashioned through the potency of Thy will. And at whatever time my pen ascribeth glory to any one of Thy names, methinks I can hear the voice of its lamentation in its remoteness from Thee, and can recognize its cry because of its separation from Thy Self. I testify that everything other than Thee is but Thy creation and is held in the hollow of Thy hand. To have accepted any act or praise from Thy creatures is but an evidence of the wonders of Thy grace and bountiful favors, and a manifestation of Thy generosity and providence.

I entreat Thee, O my Lord, by Thy Most Great Name whereby Thou didst separate light from fire, and truth from denial, to send down upon me and upon such of my loved ones as are in my company the good of this world and of the next. Supply us, then, with Thy wondrous gifts that are hid from the eyes of men. Thou art, verily, the Fashioner of all creation. No God is there but Thee, the Almighty, the All-Glorious, the Most High.[15]

I bear witness, O my God, that Thou hast created me to know Thee and to worship Thee. I testify, at this moment, to my powerlessness and to Thy might, to my poverty and to Thy wealth.

There is none other God but Thee, the Help in Peril, the Self-Subsisting.[16]

O my God! O my God! This, Thy servant, hath advanced towards Thee, is passionately wandering in the desert of Thy love, walking in the path of Thy service, anticipating Thy favors, hoping for Thy bounty, relying upon Thy kingdom, and intoxicated by the wine of Thy gift. O my God! Increase the fervor of his affection for Thee, the constancy of his praise of Thee, and the ardor of his love for Thee.

Verily, Thou art the Most Generous, the Lord of grace abounding. There is no other God but Thee, the Forgiving, the Merciful.[17]

2

Using the Power of Prayer

*The power of prayer is very great, and attracts
the Divine confirmations.*
—SHOGHI EFFENDI

Our understanding of prayer has developed over the ages. Every time God has sent a great Prophet to the world, we have learned more about the power of prayer. The prayers we say are not for God's benefit, but for ours. We pray, not because God needs to hear the words that we pray, but because we need to hear ourselves expressing our love for God and inviting Him into our lives. We have learned that prayer isn't just a set of words to go along with a particular rite or ritual. Prayer is not just the garment worn on the Sabbath—it is the garb of everyday life. Prayer is as personal and individual as we are, and God receives not just the words we offer, but our actions and thoughts as well.

At the dawn of every day [the true seeker] should commune with God, and with all his soul persevere in the quest of his Beloved. He should consume every wayward thought with the flame of His loving mention, and, with the swiftness of lightning, pass by all else save Him.[1]

The state of prayer is the best of conditions, for man is then associating with God. Prayer verily bestoweth life.[2]

Pray to and seek assistance from God, and . . . supplicate and implore His aid.[3]

Prayer helps to connect us with God. His abiding love surrounds us at all times, but we have to take the initiative through prayer to experience it and develop our relationship with Him. Regardless of the forms it may take, the most fundamental element of prayer is the remembrance of God. In whatever way we choose to do it, the most significant thing we can do is to remember our Creator.

The impulse to prayer is a natural one, springing from man's love to God.[4]

The core of religious faith is that mystic feeling which unites man with God. This state of spiritual communion can be brought about and maintained by means of meditation and prayer.[5]

Our prayerful words can take many various forms. Whether the words are whispered or sung, recited from memory or spoken spontaneously; whether the prayers entreat or praise, beseech or supplicate, God hears them all. There is, however, a special power in reading aloud or reciting the words revealed by God—that is, the words of the Prophets. This is why they are chanted and sung in every language around the world. They are the best lyrics to the music of life, for they have a powerful, transforming effect on our souls.

Intone, O My servant, the verses of God that have been received by thee, as intoned by them who have drawn nigh unto Him, that the sweetness of thy melody may kindle thine own soul, and attract the hearts of all men. Whoso reciteth, in the privacy of his chamber, the verses revealed by God, the scattering angels of the Almighty shall scatter abroad the fragrance of the words uttered by his mouth, and shall cause the heart of every righteous man to throb. Though he may, at first, remain unaware of its effect, yet the virtue of the grace vouchsafed unto him must needs sooner or later exercise its influence upon his soul. Thus have the mysteries of the Revelation of God been decreed by virtue of the Will of Him Who is the Source of power and wisdom.[6]

Our prayerful actions are the implementation of our prayerful words. Everything we do is seen by God. Eventually our prayerfulness is reflected in our daily lives. When looking for indications of our own spiritual growth, good deeds are always more convincing than good words. They are the proof of our sincerity and progress. Ultimately we judge ourselves by what we do, not by what we say we will do. In the minds of others our deeds will be remembered long after our words dissipate into nothingness. Prayerful actions are our legacy to the world. Bahá'í scripture states,

Let deeds, not words, be your adorning.[7]

Prayer need not be in words, but rather in thought and attitude. But if this love and this desire are lacking, it is useless to try to force them. Words without love mean nothing.[8]

There is no better legacy than selfless acts of loving-kindness; they uplift the spiritual condition of humankind, and no prayer for the world could be more powerful than this. The effects of our loving-kindness endure well beyond the days of our own lives.

The most acceptable prayer is the one offered with the utmost spirituality and radiance; its prolongation hath not been and is not beloved by God. The more detached and the purer the prayer, the more acceptable is it in the presence of God.[9]

The prayerful condition is the best of all conditions, for man in such a state communeth with God. . . . Indeed, prayer imparteth life.[10]

Our prayerful thoughts are our inner voices ascending to a higher realm. They are the whispered prayers of the heart to which God is always listening. Our inner thoughts, in addition to what we say and what we do, are part of our personal identity because they express the condition of our soul and influence its development. This is why we pray and meditate—to help us develop a deep sense of love and reverence for our Creator in our thoughts and to make such thoughts the foundation of who we are. Prayer and the remembrance of God are the most effective ways of doing this. Reverence is an attitude manifested in the heart long before it can be heard in our voices or seen in our behavior.

When all three of these aspects of prayerfulness—our thoughts, our words, and our actions—are brought together and harmonized, we begin to reflect the true reality of our inner spiritual being. When we have sincerely turned to God, prayerfulness becomes our state of being. The entirety of our lives can be seen as one seamless and enduring prayer.

Through the faculty of meditation man attains to eternal life; through it he receives the breath of the Holy Spirit—the bestowal of the Spirit is given in reflection and meditation.[11]

Our prayers sometimes focus on the external circumstances of our lives and the things we desire. It seems only natural to request of God the things we lack. However, there may be a difference between what we want and what we need. We may think that these are the same, but often they are not. The difficulty is that we may have some idea of what we want, but we probably have no idea of what we really need. Only God knows this. We can wish for something that, in the end, is detrimental to us. Because of this, our Creator should not be viewed in the same light as a fairy godmother. God is not in the business of wish fulfillment. Bahá'í scripture explains,

> The true worshipper, while praying, should endeavour not so much to ask God to fulfil his wishes and desires, but rather to adjust these and make them conform to the Divine Will. Only through such an attitude can one derive that feeling of inner peace and contentment which the power of prayer alone can confer.[12]

When we pray, we should strive to remember that it is our duty to align our will to God's and not God's to ours. If we are humble in our requests and condition them upon their conformity to the will of God, this will be most conducive to our spiritual growth. There are many things to pray for, but the most beneficial things are those which awaken our spiritual being and advance our spiritual journey.

Selected Prayers from Bahá'í Scripture

O Lord! Unto Thee I repair for refuge, and toward all Thy signs I set my heart.

O Lord! Whether traveling or at home, and in my occupation or in my work, I place my whole trust in Thee.

Grant me then Thy sufficing help so as to make me independent of all things, O Thou Who art unsurpassed in Thy mercy!

Bestow upon me my portion, O Lord, as Thou pleasest, and cause me to be satisfied with whatsoever Thou hast ordained for me.

Thine is the absolute authority to command.[13]

Make firm our steps, O Lord, in Thy path and strengthen Thou our hearts in Thine obedience. Turn our faces toward the beauty of Thy oneness, and gladden our bosoms with the signs of Thy divine unity. Adorn our bodies with the robe of Thy bounty, and remove from our eyes the veil of sinfulness, and give us the chalice of Thy grace; that the essence of all beings may sing Thy praise before the vision of Thy grandeur. Reveal then Thyself, O Lord, by Thy merciful utterance and the mystery of Thy divine being, that the holy ecstasy of prayer may fill our souls—a prayer that shall rise above words and letters and transcend the murmur of syllables and sounds—that all things may be merged into nothingness before the revelation of Thy splendor.

Lord! These are servants that have remained fast and firm in Thy Covenant and Thy Testament, that have held fast unto the cord of constancy in Thy Cause and clung unto the hem of the robe of Thy grandeur. Assist them, O Lord, with Thy grace, confirm them with Thy power and strengthen their loins in obedience to Thee.

Thou art the Pardoner, the Gracious.[14]

O God, my God! Thou art my Hope and my Beloved, my highest Aim and Desire! With great humbleness and entire devotion I pray to Thee to make me a minaret of Thy love in Thy land, a lamp of Thy knowledge among Thy creatures, and a banner of divine bounty in Thy dominion.

Number me with such of Thy servants as have detached themselves from everything but Thee, have sanctified themselves from the transitory things of this world, and have freed themselves from the promptings of the voicers of idle fancies.

Let my heart be dilated with joy through the spirit of confirmation from Thy kingdom, and brighten my eyes by beholding the hosts of divine assistance descending successively upon me from the kingdom of Thine omnipotent glory.

Thou art, in truth, the Almighty, the All-Glorious, the All-Powerful.[15]

3

Growing Spiritually

Spirituality is the greatest of God's gifts.
—'Abdu'l-Bahá

The ultimate purpose of life is often difficult to fathom. We may say, as a matter of faith, that we believe God has a plan for our lives; but if we are honest with ourselves, much of the time we may see only chaos, confusion, and disappointment. Sometimes, no matter how great our faith may be, things seem to get worse far more rapidly than we can ever make them better. Inevitably at some point we ask ourselves what the purpose of this life is. We wonder why we are here. Within the great scheme of things, we really would like to know what it all means and what God has planned for us personally, especially when we find ourselves surrounded by challenges and difficulties.

The problem is that any explanation we come up with seems rather unsatisfactory. It doesn't explain the meaning of what *we* are experiencing or the purpose of *our* lives. Getting older helps. The more we mature, the more we understand about the ways of this world. We learn to see beyond chaos to the underlying order of things; we replace confusion with the power of reason and find fulfillment in what we do for others rather than disappointment in what others don't do for us. When we can look back on our lives, we can see more fully what we could not comprehend while it was happening to us as youngsters. Perhaps the greatest advantage of growing older is hindsight.

With hindsight we can compare who we used to be with who we are now; we can see how our basic outlook has changed over a lifetime. Looking back on the lessons of life, we can see that learning new things was ultimately not as difficult as unlearning old things. When we were young we made assumptions about life and the world, which we later came to see as overly simplistic, woefully inadequate, or just downright wrong. These realizations are all signs of spiritual growth, but seeing ourselves become wiser than we once were doesn't necessarily lead to understanding our ultimate purpose in life.

To achieve this it may be useful to look at a different part of our lives. Before we were born we spent about forty weeks in a different world— a small, confined space separated from this world by a few thin layers of tissue. The purpose of these layers was to protect us until we were ready to emerge. This was the womb-world; in a sense it was a world within a world. Now let's ask the same questions again, but this time in retrospect. Instead of asking, What is the purpose of this life? Why are we here? Let's ask, What was the purpose of that prenatal life? Why were we there? These questions are remarkably easier to answer because it is clear that the purpose of our prenatal lives was to prepare us for this world, the world outside the womb.

In the womb, we had everything that we required: warmth, sustenance, and shelter. And, through the placenta and umbilical cord, everything we needed came to us without request or effort, without choice or volition. It was a wonderful little world where everything was given to us. Even though we spent all of our time preparing to leave that small world, we were unaware that this was what we were doing. There was no reason to think of leaving because we were perfectly fine where we were. And besides, we were completely unaware that any other place existed. We didn't know that there was a vast world all around us just outside the womb, or that it had always been there. We couldn't know; we had not yet developed the sensory equipment to perceive it properly.

Within the womb, we were growing things we had little use for in that environment, and the reason for this was beyond our comprehension at the time. We were growing hands, feet, and eyes in a place where there was little to hold, no place to walk, and nothing to see. Enveloped in that watery environment, we were growing lungs in a place without air to breathe. Even though we remained unaware of the process of growth and development, we were becoming less and less suited to remain where we were and more and more prepared for where we were going. Things were getting progressively tighter, and our movements were becoming more restricted. Eventually we completely outgrew the womb.

Only from our present vantage point can we understand the ultimate purpose of life in the womb and see that, in a sense, we had to die out of one world to be born into the next. While we were in the womb, we could not imagine leaving behind the umbilical cord, placenta, and amniotic fluid of the womb, which were far more important to our survival than the strange appendages we were growing. Imagine what would have happened if we could have chosen not to develop these limbs and members because they seemed useless in the womb. We would be handicapped at the very least—perhaps even unable to survive in this world.

Similarly the purpose of this earthly world beyond the womb is to provide the opportunities we need to develop those spiritual faculties that will best serve us in the life hereafter. We can make choices about which virtues—that is, which spiritual faculties—we will develop. These virtues may at times seem to be of little use in this world, but they will be vital in the next.

———————————

The purpose of the one true God in manifesting Himself is to summon all mankind to truthfulness and sincerity, to piety and trustworthiness, to resignation and submissiveness to the Will of God, to forbearance and kindliness, to uprightness and wisdom. His object is to array every man with the mantle of a saintly character, and to adorn him with the ornament of holy and goodly deeds.[1]

Man—the true man—is soul, not body.[2]

———————————

The remembrance of God in prayer, in attitude, and in action will help us acquire these virtues of character. With effort and time, they grow and become more substantial, eventually becoming manifest in everything we do. The virtues we manifest and cultivate shape our identity and character while we are still in this world and can greatly assist us in dealing with life's challenges. In the spiritual realm beyond this physical life these virtues define who we are. Metaphorically they are our spiritual limbs and members.

It is only by the breath of the Holy Spirit that spiritual development can come about. No matter how the material world may progress, no matter how splendidly it may adorn itself, it can never be anything but a lifeless body unless the soul is within, for it is the soul that animates the body; the body alone has no real significance. Deprived of the blessings of the Holy Spirit the material body would be inert.[3]

Love is heaven's kindly light, the Holy Spirit's eternal breath that vivifieth the human soul. . . . Love is the one means that ensureth true felicity both in this world and the next. Love is the light that guideth in darkness, the living link that uniteth God with man, that assureth the progress of every illumined soul.[4]

In our spiritual journey to attain the attributes of God, our souls either consciously or unconsciously seek their Creator. It is instinctive for the soul to do this. This instinct manifests itself as a feeling deep within us that something is missing from our lives, and the longer we live the more we notice it. We look around at the world and ask ourselves if this is all there is, and we may begin to suspect that what we seek is not in this world.

The spiritually learned must be characterized by both inward and outward perfections; they must possess a good character, an enlightened nature, a pure intent, as well as intellectual power, brilliance and discernment, intuition, discretion and foresight, temperance, reverence, and a heartfelt fear of God. For an unlit candle, however great in diameter and tall, is no better than a barren palm tree or a pile of dead wood.[5]

We must strive unceasingly and without rest to accomplish the development of the spiritual nature in man. . . . For the body of man is accidental; it is of no importance. The time of its disintegration will inevitably come. But the spirit of man is essential and, therefore, eternal.[6]

We may set many goals for ourselves in life, but the most significant is the goal of finding out why we are here. In the beginning we search without any idea of what we might be seeking; we may not even realize that we are searching. We wander about in every direction, looking for a trace of the thing for which our souls long. This search can take many forms, particularly if we do not realize what we are looking for. We may find ourselves devoted to an important social issue or problem, giving it a central place in our lives and focusing on it to the exclusion of all else. Or we may pursue a less altruistic path and put our energy and devotion into things that are more self-indulgent and hedonistic— things that distract our attention from our craving for God's love. We may travel down many paths, make many false starts, and find ourselves at many a dead end, but if we are learning from the journey, we grow spiritually from all of these experiences. In seeking traces of our Creator we learn patience. This is important to acquire because the search takes as long as it takes. Finding the Source of our existence is like a treasure hunt—there can be mishaps along the way and the map is not always clear, but with patience, ingenuity, and effort, the treasure can eventually be found.

Spiritual progress is through the breaths of the Holy Spirit and is the awakening of the conscious soul of man to perceive the reality of Divinity. Material

progress ensures the happiness of the human world.
Spiritual progress ensures the happiness and eternal
continuance of the soul.[7]

When the time is right, through the grace of God, we at last find our Creator. The process by which this happens is different for each person, reflecting the many ways that we can receive God's love and guidance. For some, constant prayer and meditation may open up a sudden path toward Him. For others, a dramatic experience in life—be it the death of a family member or the birth of a child—may flip that switch. And for some, being of service to others may connect them to God. Whatever the path, we rejoice, for we have found the love of God. We no longer wander aimlessly but direct our steps toward our heart's desire. We find ourselves filled with love, and we discover that the more we love God, the more we feel God's love for us. Little by little, as Bahá'í scripture suggests, we come to understand that God's love was always there, waiting for us to open ourselves to it:

Love Me, that I may love thee. If thou lovest Me not, My love can in no wise reach thee. Know this, O servant.[8]

That part of our spiritual being which was latent within us awakens and begins to develop, and we draw closer to God. Eventually we become consumed in our love for God. From this we begin to know the meaning of true love. Bahá'í scripture describes this state of being:

> Those souls whose inner being is lit by the love of God are even as spreading rays of light, and they shine out like stars of holiness in a pure and crystalline sky. For true love, real love, is the love of God, and this is sanctified beyond the notions and imaginings of men.[9]

Eventually we may begin to compare what we feel within us with what we see around us. More than ever, we notice the disparity and we are not content. We may feel that this world is not a very spiritual place, for it seems to lack the love we hold in our hearts. The cruelty, injustice, and suffering we see around us become intolerable, like never before. We cannot understand their purpose, and we may ask ourselves why God allows these things to happen. There doesn't seem to be an answer to this question, and even in the midst of love, whenever there is no answer, there is doubt. However, the question itself reveals something of the limitations of the one who asks, because it implies that God is somehow indifferent. And we know this is not the case. As we grow spiritually, we begin to ask better questions. We ask, Who has caused the cruelty, injustice, and suffering in the world?

The answer is that humankind has caused it and allowed it to happen. God has given us free will to make choices, and we have chosen at times to be cruel, unjust, and indifferent rather than kind, equitable, and caring. We come to realize that we are not alone in the process of spiritual growth and that we all have different lessons to learn:

> The only real difference that exists between people is that they are at various stages of development. Some are imperfect—these must be brought to perfection. Some are asleep— they must be awakened; some are negligent— they must be roused; but one and all are the children of God. Love them all with your whole heart; no one is a stranger to the other, all are friends.[10]

At this stage in our spiritual journey, doubt is gradually replaced with understanding. We begin to see that the will of God encompasses more than just love, that there is much more to learn than this. The pain inherent in love must be tempered with knowledge; we must pass beyond blind faith toward a more educated and informed faith in which we are able to reconcile the nature and limitations of this world. Bahá'í scripture exhorts us to move on to this stage, saying,

Pass beyond the baser stages of doubt and rise to the exalted heights of certainty. Open the eye of truth, that thou mayest behold the veilless Beauty and exclaim: Hallowed be the Lord, the most excellent of all creators![11]

In the process, we acquire new concepts and a spiritual vocabulary, which allow us to begin to understand why things happen and not merely how they happen. The spiritual journey requires more than just direction; we not only need to know where we are going but also why we are going there. The reason for the spiritual journey is to discover the will of God.

At some point we arrive at the stage of serendipity, in which we see traces of God in all things. We understand that, from the smallest to the largest, everything in the universe is held together by the love of God. Our initial search has yielded not just the discovery of one thing but of all things: the Divine Unity. Where there was once understanding, now there is certitude. We become aware of the nuances and subtleties around us. We realize that there are no coincidences—only the will of God. We see the circle of cause and effect, consequence and ramification; we begin to realize how all things in God's creation are interconnected. We are able to look back on the path of our own spiritual growth and realize that in ignorance we used to try to bend God's will to ours. In the past, when we said all things are possible with God, we meant that the things we wished and desired were possible because God loved us so much that He should grant our wishes. We can see how we have progressed in our understanding. Now we believe that all things are possible within God's will, and we find ourselves receiving gifts beyond our wants and desires, blessings beyond measure.

Sooner or later, as our spiritual growth continues, we come to the stage in which we find true contentment with the will of God. We see that God's will is sufficient, and we begin to attune our will to His. We want to do what is pleasing to God, and our concept of happiness is gradually transformed; instead of feeling that our pleasure depends on having things conform to our own will and understanding, we see that there is only one true will in the universe and that it has made ample provision for us all.

Contentment allows us to truly behold God's creation, including our own selves. We discover that the soul is more wondrous than we ever thought it could be, more wondrous than we could ever know. It is endowed with the capacity to fathom ever deeper the relevance of the seen and the unseen, to continue forever to discern more clearly the complexity of God's creation and how it is interwoven with God's will. We stand in awe and wonder as we recognize the evidences of God in the physical cosmos and in the infinity of the spiritual universe—the endless worlds of God. With each stage of our spiritual growth and development, we uncover more and more of that which was latent within us. Along the path of our spiritual journey we remove, one by one, the veils that keep us from seeing our true selves; for buried within the soul is the capacity to search, to love, to know, to align our will with God's, to be content, to feel wonder, and more. Gradually we acquire and refine more and more of these virtues until the self is merged in the ocean of God's light, the virtues of the soul become aligned with the attributes of God, and our will becomes indistinguishable from God's will.

Some of these stages of spiritual growth may seem more familiar than others, just as the experiences of the past and present are more familiar to us than experiences yet to come. However, all of them are woven into the fabric of our spiritual lives. For each of us the advancement of the soul along the pathway of eternity has already begun. We may go through these stages in any order, sometimes even all at once. We will go through them again and again because we are never "done." That is OK. The important thing is that we are growing spiritually, continually perfecting ourselves and drawing ever closer to God.

Selected Prayers from Bahá'í Scripture

From the sweet-scented streams of Thine eternity give me to drink, O my God, and of the fruits of the tree of Thy being enable me to taste, O my Hope! From the crystal springs of Thy love suffer me to quaff, O my Glory, and beneath the shadow of Thine everlasting providence let me abide, O my Light! Within the meadows of Thy nearness, before Thy presence, make me able to roam, O my Beloved, and at the right hand of the throne of Thy mercy, seat me, O my Desire! From the fragrant breezes of Thy joy let a breath pass over me, O my Goal, and into the heights of the paradise of Thy reality let me gain admission, O my Adored One! To the melodies of the dove of Thy oneness suffer me to hearken, O Resplendent One, and through the spirit of Thy power and Thy might quicken me, O my Provider! In the spirit of Thy love keep me steadfast, O my Succorer, and in the path of Thy good-pleasure set firm my steps, O my Maker! Within the garden of Thine immortality, before Thy countenance, let me abide for ever, O Thou Who art merciful unto me, and upon the seat of Thy glory stablish me, O Thou Who art my Possessor! To the heaven of Thy loving-kindness lift me up, O my Quickener, and unto the Daystar of Thy guidance lead me, O Thou my Attractor! Before the revelations of Thine invisible spirit summon me to be present, O Thou Who art my Origin and my Highest Wish, and unto the essence of the fragrance of Thy beauty, which Thou wilt manifest, cause me to return, O Thou Who art my God!

Potent art Thou to do what pleasest Thee. Thou art, verily, the Most Exalted, the All-Glorious, the All-Highest.[12]

Create in me a pure heart, O my God, and renew a tranquil conscience within me, O my Hope! Through the spirit of power confirm Thou me in Thy Cause, O my Best-Beloved, and by the light of Thy glory reveal unto me Thy path, O Thou the Goal of my desire! Through the power of Thy transcendent might lift me up unto the heaven of Thy holiness, O Source of my being, and by the breezes of Thine eternity gladden me, O Thou Who art my God! Let Thine everlasting melodies breathe tranquillity on me, O my Companion, and let the riches of Thine ancient countenance deliver me from all except Thee, O my Master, and let the tidings of the revelation of Thine incorruptible Essence bring me joy, O Thou Who art the most manifest of the manifest and the most hidden of the hidden![13]

O God, guide me, protect me, make of me a shining lamp and a brilliant star. Thou art the Mighty and the Powerful.[14]

4

Dealing with Life's Tests

Tests are benefits from God. . . . Grief and sorrow do not come to us by chance, they are sent to us by the Divine Mercy for our own perfecting.
—'ABDU'L-BAHÁ

The narrative of our life-story is punctuated with difficulties. While we are going through the difficulties, it is hard to see any purpose in them. But when we look at them in retrospect, often we can see that the challenges we face are the catalyst for spiritual growth. Irrespective of their size, all difficulties test the limits of our spiritual abilities and enable us to progress from one level of development to the next.

Some problems seem simple and are dealt with at once, while others linger unresolved and revisit us repeatedly throughout our lives. Some problems are endemic and so great that they may span several generations and cannot be resolved within just one lifetime or by one person alone. Other difficulties seem to be custom designed especially for us for the sole purpose of improving our character.

Regardless of the kinds of difficulties we experience, it will be helpful to realize that we learn some of life's most valuable lessons primarily from the efforts we make and not necessarily from the immediate outcome of the events around us. We are not alone in this world, and the outcome of things is often outside our power to control. However, our willingness to deal with challenges and learn what we can from them is an essential factor in our spiritual growth. This is a theme that comes up again and again in Bahá'í scripture.

---

*Men who suffer not, attain no perfection. The plant
most pruned by the gardeners is that one which, when
summer comes, will have the most beautiful blossoms
and the most abundant fruit.*[1]

We may often ask ourselves why we must
suffer, wondering if there is any wisdom to it. It
can be very difficult to see suffering as anything
more than a difficult ordeal, let alone as the
best means by which we can grow and improve
ourselves spiritually. Such an attitude initially
may strike us as somewhat masochistic. Yet if
we think about it, it's easy to see that just as
the tree pruned most by the gardener thrives
best and yields the most fruit, so do tests and
trials improve us spiritually. Bahá'í scripture
states,

The mind and spirit of man advance when he
is tried by suffering. The more the ground is
ploughed the better the seed will grow, the
better the harvest will be. Just as the plough
furrows the earth deeply, purifying it of weeds
and thistles, so suffering and tribulation free
man from the petty affairs of this worldly life
until he arrives at a state of complete detachment. His attitude in this world will be that of
divine happiness. Man is, so to speak, un-

ripe: the heat of the fire of suffering will mature him. Look back to the times past and you will find that the greatest men have suffered most.[2]

Thus suffering has a spiritual purpose. By approaching it as a learning experience and growing from it, we become better human beings. It is comforting to know, however, that God will never burden a soul beyond its capacity to endure. We are assured in Bahá'í scripture that God "will never deal unjustly with any one, neither will He task a soul beyond its power. He, verily, is the Compassionate, the All-Merciful."[3] Further, "There is no doubt that difficulties will always arise; but if met in the spirit of earnest and selfless devotion and purity of motive all problems will be solved and we shall emerge from every difficulty spiritually stronger and wiser."[4]

Should prosperity befall thee, rejoice not, and should abasement come upon thee, grieve not, for both shall pass away and be no more.[5]

Sorrow not if, in these days and on this earthly plane, things contrary to your wishes have been ordained and manifested by God, for days of blissful joy, of heavenly delight, are assuredly in store for you.[6]

We become stronger and wiser by two closely related means: personal trial and error and the observation of other people's trials and errors. In both cases we learn not only from successes but also from mistakes. Mistakes can be painful experiences, but they are also very effective teachers. This fact is often overlooked in a society that overemphasizes the value of material success. Our desire for this kind of success, like our belief in the pursuit of happiness, is not wrong in itself, but it can easily distract us from the primary purpose of life. Dealing with the difficulties that come our way is much more spiritually beneficial than striving for the type of success that is measured in prestige, power, or wealth. By their nature prestige, power, and wealth are relative measurements that require us to compare what we have with what others have. There is nothing inherently wrong with having these things unless they come between us and God. But having more fame, more clout, and more money than others can easily become the goal of life. When this happens we tend to deal with others competitively and see problem-solving as the means to personal and material gain.

Do not grieve at the afflictions and calamities that have befallen thee. All calamities and afflictions have been created for man so that he may spurn this mor-

tal world—a world to which he is much attached. When he experienceth severe trials and hardships, then his nature will recoil and he will desire the eternal realm— a realm which is sanctified from all afflictions and calamities.[7]

This way of thinking can be very alluring. The skills of problem-solving are sometimes conveniently packaged as a set of strategies and marketed as formulas for success. The desire for shortcuts is a phenomenon of the times in which we live and, sadly, has become the basis of many self-help programs. Such strategies selectively gloss over some of the complexities of life and tend to require that we ignore the rest of reality as we examine a single aspect of our lives. They often focus on a particular social environment such as school, the workplace, or interpersonal relationships and are founded on the assumption that power overcomes problems and that some outside agency is the likely cause of our problems rather than our own behavior. Success is often defined as the ability to impose our will on others and the courage to take control of the destiny we make for ourselves. These strategies erroneously claim that if a particular formula is followed, we will have control over the outcome. They generally overlook the role God plays in solving our problems. Prayer is described in the Bahá'í writings as "essentially a communion between man and God" that "transcends all ritualistic forms and formulae."[8] If we ignore God's role in testing and refining our characters, we are left with relying on formulas that tend to work only within certain narrow contexts and only for a short time. Eventually it becomes clear that this kind of success has its price and that such strategies are not very conducive to spiritual growth. In fact, they may actually tend to bring out the worst in us.

But still we naturally search for effective ways to deal with our difficulties. There are a couple of aspects of problems that are often overlooked. Whenever a problem arises, the first thing to do is to check our emotional responses to it. Our attitudes toward the problem can often become a greater problem than the problem itself and can hamper our spiritual growth. This is inherent in every difficulty we encounter, no matter how old we may be. Controlling our response is a practical spiritual skill that can be learned, and its effects can be far-reaching. If we are parents it is one of the most helpful skills we can teach our children.

An example of how this skill is used will illustrate its value. Let's say that one day a child comes home in tears and asks for help in solving a problem she has at school. She tells her parents that children on the playground are taunting her, spreading rumors, and accusing her of things she didn't do. It is clear that she is distressed by what the children are saying, and she asks her parents to help. Her parents know this is a problem that at some point will probably involve a trip to the school and a frank discussion with a school administrator. But first there is something they feel they must do for their daughter: They want to help her understand that she has a choice in how she responds to the problem.

The parents find a creative way to demonstrate this. They remember that there is a container of leftovers festering at the back of the refrigerator. It's really hideous, slimy, and covered with mold. They get it out and offer it to their daughter, saying, "Here, take this. It's ours, but we want you to have it." The daughter declines. The parents repeat, "No, really, we want you to have it." The daughter puts her hands behind her back and looks at her parents incredulously. Now the parents can explain the object of the lesson. They explain that until someone accepts the container of furry slime, it belongs to whoever is trying to give it away. They explain that the same principle holds true for taunts, accusations, and insults. If we don't accept them, they are not ours and we do not have to internalize them. We have the right to say, "No, thank you." This doesn't make the taunting go away, of course, but we don't have to be upset by it. The lesson here is about practicing detachment and controlling ourselves, not others. Often we have no direct control over our circumstances, but we certainly have a choice in how we respond to them.

Our greatest efforts must be directed towards detachment from the things of the world; we must strive to become more spiritual, more luminous, to follow the counsel of the Divine Teaching, to serve the cause of unity and true equality, to be merciful, to reflect the love of the Highest on all men, so that the light of the Spirit shall be apparent in all our deeds, to the end that all humanity shall be united, the stormy sea thereof calmed, and all rough waves disappear from off the surface of life's ocean henceforth unruffled and peaceful.[9]

The first and perhaps most important lesson the daughter can learn is not to become ruffled by others' behavior. This is not easily achieved, but it should be a goal no matter how old we are, because we will find similar playgrounds throughout our lives. As children and often as adults, those who taunt do it to get a reaction because they believe that there are two kinds of people: victimizers and victims, winners and losers. They have acquired a mentality which is based on the belief that if they don't want to be the one, then they must become the other. We have all experienced this, and the children on the playground know that the easiest way to avoid being taunted is to join the taunters and victimize others. And so it continues. Generation after generation, the children have learned the rules by observation.

As adults, however, we are challenged to unlearn much of what we assimilated as children. As parents we must find a way to teach our children to be neither victims nor victimizers, neither passive nor aggressive. In so doing, our children learn to rise above the standards that society sets for them, becoming manifestations of true justice. Bahá'í scripture states, "no man can attain his true station except through his justice."[10]

You must manifest complete love and affection toward all mankind. Do not exalt yourselves above others, but consider all as your equals, recognizing them as the servants of one God. Know that God is compassionate toward all; therefore, love all from the depths of your hearts . . . be filled with love for every race, and be kind toward the people of all nationalities. Never speak disparagingly of others, but praise without distinction. Pollute not your tongues by speaking evil of another. Recognize your enemies as friends, and consider those who wish you evil as the wishers of good. . . . Act in such a way that your heart may be free

*from hatred. Let not your heart be offended with any-
one. If some one commits an error and wrong toward
you, you must instantly forgive him.... Turn all your
thoughts toward bringing joy to hearts.*[11]

To achieve our true station and practice justice is a tall order and will be extremely difficult
to achieve without prayer. Prayer has the power
not only to transform our fundamental attitudes
toward difficulties, but also to assist us in thinking clearly and identifying the causes of problems. Simply remaining unruffled isn't enough.
If we desire to make the world a better place,
we will have to help solve the problems we encounter. This requires the ability to differenti-
ate between symptoms and causes, because
until we determine the root of a problem we cannot devise a plan of action for its solution. Undoubtedly the school administrator in the playground scenario will probably attempt to treat
the symptom. But simply telling the children to
stop being cruel or even threatening punishment
will not be sufficient to eradicate the behavior.
The behavior is not the cause of the problem;
usually the real difficulty lies in the beliefs and
attitudes that gave rise to the behavior.

As children, we learned our attitudes, beliefs,
values, and perceptions by watching the behavior of our parents and peers. Despite the con-
tradictory advice we may occasionally have been
given, the only reality we knew was the example

of what we saw. This is logically accepted as the standard. So when the school administrator calls an offending child into the office and admonishes him with mere words that are not supported by personal example, nothing is likely to change. The only lesson the child is likely to learn is to be more careful in his cruelty. After all, the child didn't see anything wrong with what he was doing; he was only following the example set by others and playing a game of winners and losers.

This taunting behavior has been the playground standard for a very long time, and it will continue to be if there is no counterexample among us to teach otherwise. A positive example is the solution to the problem. Despite whatever pronouncement the school may make on the subject, the daughter who learns to say "No, thank you" and becomes a positive example can be the most powerful agent of change on the playground. With a kind, sincere, and calm demeanor, and with an idea of the task at hand, this child can influence what games get played by demonstrating a new kind of behavior. It may take a long time for the cruelty to disappear, perhaps many years. But we don't just solve problems for ourselves—we solve them for the generations of little girls and boys yet unborn.

The Almighty hath tried, and will continue to try, His servants, so that light may be distinguished from dark-

ness, truth from falsehood, right from wrong, guidance from error, happiness from misery, and roses from thorns.[12]

Be thou neither grieved nor despondent over what hath come to pass. This trouble overtook thee as thou didst walk the path of God, wherefore it should bring thee joy.[13]

While a man is happy he may forget his God; but when grief comes and sorrows overwhelm him, then will he remember his Father who is in Heaven, and who is able to deliver him.[14]

Patience and acquiring a longer view of things will do a great deal for us in coping with difficulties. If we put our faith in God at all times, good or bad, we will find ourselves better able to manifest these qualities. If we view our lives as a collaborative effort between God and ourselves, then it becomes easier to see that there are things which are our responsibilities and others that only God can perform. It is a little bit like moving a stalled vehicle. Our job is to push the vehicle ahead while God steers. If we don't take action and work to overcome our problems, we may not be able to see what God is doing to help us and steer us in the right direction. Metaphorically, God can be turning the steering wheel, but if the vehicle is not moving because we are not putting forth enough effort, we will not see the guidance and direction our Creator is offering. Turning to God will always help to solve our difficulties. Prayer has the ability to overcome the inertia of the stalled vehicle of our lives.

Bahá'ís all over the world find comfort in using the following prayer from Bahá'í scripture to invoke God's help during difficult times:

Is there any Remover of difficulties save God? Say: Praised be God! He is God! All are His servants, and all abide by His bidding![15]

When difficulties arise in our emotional and physical well-being we must seek God's help. Turning to God helps dispel our sadness. Prayer has the power to help us change our attitudes about the circumstances that come our way. Another prayer from Bahá'í scripture can help to change our sorrow to joy:

O God! Refresh and gladden my spirit. Purify my heart. Illumine my powers. I lay all my affairs in Thy hand. Thou art my Guide and my Refuge. I will no longer be sorrowful and grieved; I will be a happy and joyful being. O God! I will no longer be full of anxiety, nor will I let trouble harass me. I will not dwell on the unpleasant things of life.

O God! Thou art more friend to me than I am to myself. I dedicate myself to Thee, O Lord.[16]

Turning to God will also help remove our afflictions. Both the physical and spiritual means of healing sickness should be practiced. We should not separate them, for they work together, and both are important. We should take advantage of the expertise of competent physicians who will endeavor to find the cause of our ailments and not merely to treat the symptoms; yet we should also turn to God in prayer as we seek to be cured. The following prayer from Bahá'í scripture can be very helpful when healing is needed:

Thy name is my healing, O my God, and remembrance of Thee is my remedy. Nearness to Thee is my hope, and love for Thee is my companion. Thy mercy to me is my healing and my succor in both this world and the world to come. Thou, verily, art the All-Bountiful, the All-Knowing, the All-Wise.[17]

Physical and mental health are closely related to spiritual well-being. Our mental responses to life move through a spectrum of emotions that deeply affect our physical being, just as an ailment to our bodies affects the functioning and clarity of our minds. Refreshing the spirit helps to remove the tarnish that sometimes clouds the mirror of the soul.

The circumstances of our lives often pose financial difficulties. Again, our attitudes toward such problems can either assist or hinder their resolution. Bahá'í scripture advises us to be generous in times of personal prosperity and thankful during times of adversity, for both conditions are temporary, and one follows the other through life. When we find ourselves struggling with adversity, it may help to remember those whose lives are full of difficulties and whose trials are continual. If we can find a way to be of service to others, it will be a great benefit to ourselves, for it will allow us to see the circumstances of others' lives and will put our own situation in perspective.

Be generous in prosperity, and thankful in adversity.[18]

Let not the happenings of the world sadden you.[19]

All the sorrow and the grief that exist come from the world of matter—the spiritual world bestows only the joy![20]

Selected Prayers from Bahá'í Scripture

Dispel my grief by Thy bounty and Thy generosity, O God, my God, and banish mine anguish through Thy sovereignty and Thy might. Thou seest me, O my God, with my face set towards Thee at a time when sorrows have compassed me on every side. I implore Thee, O Thou Who art the Lord of all being, and overshadowest all things visible and invisible, by Thy Name whereby Thou hast subdued the hearts and the souls of men, and by the billows of the Ocean of Thy mercy and the splendors of the Daystar of Thy bounty, to number me with them whom nothing whatsoever hath deterred from setting their faces toward Thee, O Thou Lord of all names and Maker of the heavens!

Thou beholdest, O my Lord, the things which have befallen me in Thy days. I entreat Thee, by Him Who is the Dayspring of Thy names and the Dawning-Place of Thine attributes, to ordain for me what will enable me to arise to serve Thee and to extol Thy virtues. Thou art, verily, the Almighty, the Most Powerful, Who art wont to answer the prayers of all men!

And, finally, I beg of Thee by the light of Thy countenance to bless my affairs, and redeem my debts, and satisfy my needs. Thou art He to Whose power and to Whose dominion every tongue hath testified, and Whose majesty and Whose sovereignty every understanding heart hath acknowledged. No God is there but Thee, Who hearest and art ready to answer.[21]

I adjure Thee by Thy might, O my God! Let no harm beset me in times of tests, and in moments of heedlessness guide my steps aright through Thine inspiration. Thou art God, potent art Thou to do what Thou desirest. No one can withstand Thy Will or thwart Thy Purpose.[22]

O Lord! Thou art the Remover of every anguish and the Dispeller of every affliction. Thou art He Who banisheth every sorrow and setteth free every slave, the Redeemer of every soul. O Lord! Grant deliverance through Thy mercy, and reckon me among such servants of Thine as have gained salvation.[23]

O my Lord, my Beloved, my Desire! Befriend me in my loneliness and accompany me in my exile. Remove my sorrow. Cause me to be devoted to Thy beauty. Withdraw me from all else save Thee. Attract me through Thy fragrances of holiness. Cause me to be associated in Thy Kingdom with those who are severed from all else save Thee, who long to serve Thy sacred threshold and who stand to work in Thy Cause. Enable me to be one of Thy maidservants who have attained to Thy good pleasure. Verily, Thou art the Gracious, the Generous.[24]

Part 2

Nurturing the Family

Note ye how easily, where unity existeth in a given family, the affairs of that family are conducted; what progress the members of that family make, how they prosper in the world.
—'ABDU'L-BAHÁ

A family is a nation in miniature. Simply enlarge the circle of the household, and you have the nation. Enlarge the circle of nations, and you have all humanity. The conditions surrounding the family surround the nation. The happenings in the family are the happenings in the life of the nation.
—'ABDU'L-BAHÁ

Undoubtedly, among the most ancient of human institutions is the family. It has always been with us, and it is etched deeply into our social psyche. Around the world, the family unit appears in many different forms, but despite these variations, it serves the same purpose, which is to satisfy our basic need to belong. The family is a complex network of relationships held together by mutual love and the reciprocity of trust and trustworthiness. It is built upon a covenant of promises offered and kept and the willingness to share what we have with each other. At its best the family is sustained by the exchange of kindnesses often too small to be noticed and too big to be forgotten. Each family is different, and when it lives up to its true nature, each family is exceptional. The unique resonance of the family is derived from the harmonious individuality of its members. It is a choir in which each of us takes turns singing the melody of the soloist and the harmony of the chorus.

From the earliest times, the institution of the family has allowed us to identify who we are by our relationships with others. The terms we find within it are inclusive and reciprocal: We are called "son" or "daughter" because we call others "mother" and "father." It is the same between aunts and nieces, uncles and nephews, brothers and sisters, wives and husbands. These relationships have been formalized by every culture of the world into complex structures of kinship that serve to define our social rights and responsibilities. Over the centuries the social systems that have arisen from these kinships may have changed, but the family unit is still the basis of social order and stability.

The institution of the family is a gift from God, and its purpose is to provide us with the foundation for society and an environment conducive to continuous spiritual growth. For these reasons, the family is held sacred in every religion; it is a holy institution for the establishment of love and affinity in the world. At the core of the family is the spiritual commitment inherent in marriage. Bahá'í scripture explains that when husband and wife both turn toward God, the Word of God brings them closer together and strengthens their relationship, producing powerful results:

> Verily, it [the Word of God] causeth the multitudes to assemble together and the remote ones to be united. Thus the husband and wife are brought into affinity, are united and harmonized, even as though they were one person. Through their mutual union, companionship and love great results are produced in the world, both material and spiritual.[1]

The social, material, and spiritual implications of the marital bond are far-reaching, both in their obligations and in their rewards. Beyond the notion of the legitimization of a long-term relationship or a mere legal contract between two individuals, true marriage is the unity that binds both partners to each other and to every other member of the family. The sacred commitment of marriage extends beyond the love, honor, and respect we show toward our mate; it is the willingness to participate in the welfare and well-being of the entire family, regardless of its structure. The institution of marriage cannot be isolated from the institution of the family. The vows we make to the former are equally applicable in the latter. We are married to the destinies of our spouse, the children we rear, and our children's children. Our lives become linked and intertwined as we nurture each other. This is true of the entire family. On many occasions we find ourselves contributing to the good fortune of our siblings and in-laws, even that of the distant relations on the fringes of our family tree. In whatever ways we are related, we share each other's lives.

The greatest benefits we can derive from being part of a family are spiritual rather than material in nature; in fact, some may argue that having a family can be a drain on our material well-being. We are blessed with the opportunity to affect and be affected by our relatives. The family is an ongoing social, economic, and spiritual development project. As we will see in the chapters ahead, it is the model and building block for communities and nations alike.

5

Building Family Unity

The unity of the family must be sustained. The injury of one shall be considered the injury of all; the comfort of each, the comfort of all; the honor of one, the honor of all.

—'Abdu'l-Bahá

It is often said that the family unit is the foundational building block of civilization. This is certainly true. However, it is helpful to remember that it is not hewn from rigid stone. The family is an organic arrangement of many interconnected and moving parts, and each part is involved in a process of growth and transformation. Any analogy we use to describe the family is bound to be simpler than the complexity inherent in the family unit, and whatever conclusion we draw about how it works does not stand for very long. This is because the family is composed of real people and not machines with preprogrammed definitive roles, despite what may be prescribed and proscribed by tradition. There are no fixed functions for its members. With each stage of our lives our roles within the family change, and the responsibilities we once had are passed along to others as we accept new ones.

The basic parameters of family structure may vary according to where we live in the world; there are several well-established and culturally defined ways of organizing people who see themselves as related. These structures are composed of long-standing ideals and social conventions and are perpetuated because we tend to replicate what is familiar and comfortable to us. No matter what form of family structure we may find ourselves in, several interrelated components are critical to its success and unity.

These include individuality, interdependence, stability, and, above all, sanctity.

Within the family there must be a place for each person's individuality to develop and thrive. The lamp of individual character needs a niche from which it may shine.

Ye must become brilliant lamps. Ye must shine as stars radiating the light of love toward all mankind.[1]

Our membership in the family should not render the light of our own personality imperceptible. To shine forth we must have enough space to explore new ideas and investigate the truth of what we discover, and we must have the acceptance of others to do so. We must be able to determine what is appropriate for ourselves while respecting the limits of a standard of propriety. If we allow each of our family members a similar space, then we accommodate everyone's need to learn, to grow, and to be significant.

The family that respects each member's individuality is a house with many niches. In such a family there is no need to try to outshine others by diminishing or extinguishing another person's light. The brilliance of our own light is sufficient to be appreciated, and we can enjoy and benefit from each other's light rather than seeking to stand alone and above all others. If we are intolerant of another's individuality and dictate that others act as we do, everyone's light is diminished. The standard of acceptable behavior and expression needs to be shared by all. If we try to impose a standard that is self-serving, arbitrary, and entirely of our own making, we may hear ourselves say things like "Not under my roof." This is not a very good means of explaining the rationale of a standard we are trying to uphold. In fact, such explanations may signal that there is no standard, only capriciousness and the need for power.

True family stability is rarely maintained by strict adherence to tradition or by attempting to do the same thing in every situation regardless of the circumstances. No matter what we do, circumstances are bound to change. Family stability is maintained by doing the reasonable thing in the midst of changing circumstances.

The ability to determine what is reasonable is the key. This requires one to see what is beneficial to one and all. This is best achieved by having a standard to which we can compare our behaviors and values. The family is like a large, slow-moving vehicle. As it advances through time, it comes across novel ideas, fresh opportunities, and new arrangements. It tries them out, and those that seem to work are incorporated into the operation of the machine. At the same time, the machine discards outmoded ideas, waning opportunities, and nonfunctional arrangements because they no longer work. The machine is composed of all the members of the family and has a sufficient critical mass of expertise and wisdom to sustain it. Without this cumulative understanding of what works and what doesn't, the machine lacks stability. Without the stability and continuity of the family structure, we find ourselves on our own.

The long, unbroken chain of family continuity is more than just a building block of society—it is civilization. The stability it provides allows science, art, and music to flourish. Keeping the family strong and spiritually focused is not only important but essential to the continuation of civilization.

The integrity of the family bond must be constantly considered, and the rights of the individual members must not be transgressed. The rights of the son, the father, the mother—none of them must be transgressed, none of them must be arbitrary. Just as the son has certain obligations to his father, the father, likewise, has certain obligations to his son. The mother, the sister and other members of the household have their certain prerogatives. All these rights and prerogatives must be conserved, yet the unity of the family must be sustained.[2]

Often the state of the family will determine the success of individual members. The family that provides a healthy, loving, united environment for individual growth serves as a strong foundation on which the individual can build. Furthermore, the family that is united in its efforts can achieve virtually any goal it sets. The members of such a family benefit from their interdependence, enabling all to prosper.

If love and agreement are manifest in a single family, that family will advance, become illumined and spiritual; but if enmity and hatred exist within it, destruction and dispersion are inevitable.[3]

It is also true that the process of disintegration in a family is doubly amplified by the absence of unity. With each successive generation mired in unresolved enmity, fewer and fewer interdependent relationships are formed within the family. A cascade of self-destruction can begin if the enmity is not replaced with love and unity. The extended family can degenerate into poorly functioning nuclear families, which can deteriorate into fragmented one-parent families, which can then degenerate into estranged individuals with little or no sense of family. It may take several generations for this process to transpire, but if it is left to run its course, the end of the family lineage is inevitable.

Consider the harmful effect of discord and dissension in a family; then reflect upon the favors and blessings which descend upon that family when unity exists among its various members.[4]

Strive to attain a station of absolute love one toward another. By the absence of love, enmity increases. By the exercise of love, love strengthens and enmities dwindle away.[5]

However, if at some point unity begins to replace enmity, the family can begin to heal and reestablish itself. The destructive process is reversed, and the benefits that are gained touch everyone from the individual to the whole world. When unity is established between spouses, the family is united; where there are united families, there can be cooperation within the community; and with concord established in the community, there can be peace and prosperity in the world.

Treat all thy friends and relatives, even strangers, with a spirit of utmost love and kindliness.[6]

Order your lives in accordance with the first principle of the divine teaching, which is love.[7]

When you love a member of your family or a compatriot, let it be with a ray of the Infinite Love! Let it be in God, and for God! Wherever you find the attributes of God love that person, whether he be of your family or of another.[8]

The family is the home, and, according to Bahá'í belief, the station of the home has been elevated to the level of a place of worship. The family is a place wherein God should be mentioned and praised often.

My home is the home of peace. My home is the home of joy and delight. My home is the home of laughter and exaltation. Whosoever enters through the portals of this home, must go out with gladsome heart. This is the home of light; whosoever enters here must become illumined.[9]

Know thou of a certainty that every house wherein the anthem of praise is raised to the Realm of Glory in celebration of the Name of God is indeed a heavenly home, and one of the gardens of delight in the Paradise of God.[10]

The family is imbued with the potential for sanctity. The home can become a holy and sacred place if the family acquires and demonstrates the love of God, a reverence for peace, and an appreciation for joy and laughter.

The family, being a human unit, must be educated according to the rules of sanctity. All the virtues must be taught the family.[11]

The family home is our first house of worship, temple, church, synagogue, or mosque. It is the first place where we hear about God and witness on a daily basis the practical application of our religious beliefs. Whether kneeling beside our bed, sitting in a quiet corner, or standing with our palms upraised, it is the place where we learn to pray. Prayer and the mention of God can make any home a house of God.

Selected Prayers from Bahá'í Scripture

Blessed is the spot, and the house, and the place, and the city, and the heart, and the mountain, and the refuge, and the cave, and the valley, and the land, and the sea, and the island, and the meadow where mention of God hath been made, and His praise glorified.[12]

O Lord! In this Most Great Dispensation Thou dost accept the intercession of children in behalf of their parents. This is one of the special infinite bestowals of this Dispensation. Therefore, O Thou kind Lord, accept the request of this Thy servant at the threshold of Thy singleness and submerge his father in the ocean of Thy grace, because this son hath arisen to render Thee service and is exerting effort at all times in the pathway of Thy love. Verily, Thou art the Giver, the Forgiver and the Kind![13]

6

Ensuring Marital Harmony

The foundation of the Kingdom of God is based upon
harmony and love, oneness, relationship
and union, not upon differences, especially
between husband and wife.
—'ABDU'L-BAHÁ

Marriage is potentially one of the most rewarding and spiritually uplifting relationships we can have here on earth. Unlike the bond between parent and child, marriage is the deliberate union of two who wish to be one, a union of choice as opposed to biology. The Bahá'í teachings attach great importance to the marital relationship, calling it "a fortress for well-being and salvation."[1] Marriage allows two independent lives to converge and coincide as we move through this life, thereby permitting us the peerless privilege of better knowing ourselves by intimately understanding our mate and building a family together. The one who becomes our beloved is our traveling companion on the pathway of spiritual growth, the one we have chosen as our helpmate along the way. To ensure that the marriage remains harmonious and the fortress sound, we must recognize that during our marital union, we will travel many different and difficult paths, but we will travel together, hand in hand.

At all times hath union and association been well-pleasing in the sight of God, and separation and dissension abhorred. Hold fast unto that which God loveth and is His command unto you. He, verily, is the All-Knowing and the All-Seeing, and He is the All-Wise Ordainer.[2]

The Lord, peerless is He, hath made woman and man to abide with each other in the closest companionship, and to be even as a single soul. They are two helpmates, two intimate friends, who should be concerned about the welfare of each other.

If they live thus, they will pass through this world with perfect contentment, bliss, and peace of heart, and become the object of divine grace and favor in the Kingdom of heaven. But if they do other than this, they will live out their lives in great bitterness. . . .

Strive, then, to abide, heart and soul, with each other as two doves in the nest, for this is to be blessed in both worlds.[3]

It is exciting to think that marriage can be anything we wish it to be, but in fact it has the potential to become even more than we can imagine. Marriage can be the place where we truly learn to love. It can be where we not only learn to love one another, but also where we learn to love the person reflected in our beloved's eyes—ourselves. Marriage provides the opportunity to love the image that we see: the reflection of our spiritual being.

The life of a married couple should resemble the life of the angels in heaven —a life full of joy and spiritual delight, a life of unity and concord, a friendship both mental and physical. . . . Their ideas and thoughts should be like the rays of the sun of truth and the radiance of the brilliant stars in the heavens. Even as two birds they should warble melodies upon the branches of the tree of fellowship and harmony. They should always be elated with joy and gladness and be a source of happiness to the hearts of others. They should set an example to their fellow-men, manifest a true and sincere love towards each other and educate their children in such a manner as to blazon the fame and glory of their family.[4]

The Bahá'í teachings point out that in addition to the spiritual union in marriage, any truly harmonious marriage must be conditioned upon two very practical social agreements: the individuals' mutual consent and attraction to one another and the subsequent approval of their union by their parents. To those of us who come from a society in which marriages are not arranged by parents, the concept of mutual consent of the couple may seem to be a non-issue. And in like manner, to those of us who are accustomed to having parents choose spouses for their children, the consent of parents is a given. However, with the rising incidence of marriage between couples with diverse backgrounds, both kinds of consent are now practical and important to have. Regardless of the age of the couple and who arranges the marriage, the husband and wife must want to be together, and their parents must approve and bless the union. Both of these elements aid the couple to bind with one another, help the marriage to endure, and build unity in the extended family by involving the parents.

The Bahá'í Teachings do not only encourage marital life, . . . but raise marriage to the status of a divine institution, its chief and sacred purpose being the perpetuation of the human race—which is the very flower of the entire creation—and its elevation to the true station destined for it by God.[5]

Every marriage is the union of two families and not merely the formation of a new and separate household. In succeeding years the couple will likely choose to start a family, which inevitably involves the grandparents, the uncles and aunts, the cousins, and so on. Building unity at the outset of a marriage provides a strong foundation for the relationship and ensures a smooth transition into the more complex elements of married life.

If the bond of marriage is to last, the seeds of love and unity must exist and must be cultivated. Love and unity transcend this life; they are spiritual qualities that we take with us on our eternal voyage. For this reason, before entering into the covenant of marriage, each partner must become fully acquainted with the character of his or her potential spouse. Bahá'í scripture gives guidance about the process by which a Bahá'í should get to know a potential spouse:

> Marriage is the commitment of the two parties one to the other, and their mutual attachment of mind and heart. Each must, however, exercise the utmost care to become thoroughly acquainted with the character of the other, that the binding covenant between them may be a tie that will endure forever. Their purpose must be this: to become loving companions and comrades and at one with each other for time and eternity.[6]

It is also imperative that both partners understand what love is and what it is not. Love is not romance, nor is it passion, though it can include both at times. Some people associate love with affection, sentiment, infatuation, devotion, rapture, ecstasy, and more. The fact that there are so many different words associated with the concept of love reveals that it is something more than the imagination can hold. Love is like electricity: It is familiar to everyone, but no one knows its true nature. Love is not merely one thing or another. It is inherent in all things, and it is that quality which holds things together.

Deal ye one with another with the utmost love and harmony, with friendliness and fellowship. . . . So powerful is the light of unity that it can illuminate the whole earth.[7]

Truly, the Lord loveth union and harmony and abhorreth separation and divorce.[8]

We often associate marriage with the romantic notion of love. We may believe in something called a "soul mate" and dream of finding that one special individual in all of the world who is right for us. This notion is a relatively recent Western invention that has been popularized in the past few centuries. Though it is wonderful on occasions like Valentine's Day and wedding anniversaries, the romantic notion of love is not a realistic foundation for a marriage. If we attempt to make this the basis of our marriage, we are bound to be disappointed, for no long-term satisfaction is possible in romantic fantasy. Romantic love is like the sudden burst of light that flares up when you light a candle; yet the candle's longevity and usefulness are dependent on its ability to burn strongly, slowly, and consistently. In marriage it is better to base our expectations on the qualities of a person's character. Liking and respecting the person whom we are actually with will provide the greatest measure of satisfaction, as will liking who we are when we are with that person.

———————

Love is unlimited, boundless, infinite! Material things are limited, circumscribed, finite. You cannot adequately express infinite love by limited means.[9]

———————

Loving the soul and the character of our mate and being comforted by our mutual loving-kindness are enduring foundations for a marital relationship. They bring out the sacred qualities that lie hidden deep within us. There is a powerful analogy in Bahá'í scripture:

O Thou kind Lord! Make Thou this marriage to bring forth coral and pearls.[10]

The analogy here is profound; precious and organic things, like coral and pearls, take time to grow. The most important results of a marriage can take a long time to develop. Over time, our lives and personal capacities are enhanced by our union as we learn to communicate, inspire, and be sensitive to each other's spiritual needs.

———————

The importance of marriage lieth in the bringing up of a richly blessed family, so that with entire glad-

97

*ness they may, even as candles, illuminate the world.
For the enlightenment of the world dependeth upon the
existence of man. If man did not exist in this world, it
would have been like a tree without fruit.*[11]

According to Bahá'í belief, one of the most important purposes of marriage is to raise a family. There is probably no greater expression of the union between two individuals than raising children together. Many couples experience a deepening love for each other as they share the joys, challenges, and responsibilities of child rearing. Unfortunately, if the foundation of the marriage is weak, child rearing and the stresses that it creates can contribute to disunity and strife. Communication, consultation, a commitment to each other, and a shared sense of purpose are essential to working through the difficult times.

Marriage gives us opportunities to expand our ability to communicate and consult effectively. We learn to listen deeply to our partner, not so much for the purpose of agreeing or disagreeing, but because we want to show our love and respect for that person and we want to discover who he or she is. By sharing our lives in this way, we learn that communication is not about who speaks the loudest, longest, or most often. It often involves not speaking at all, but rather listening to each other attentively. We find that we can consult in a frank and loving manner as we discuss what lies ahead and together choose the kind of future we want to have. In marriage we learn that compromise—where one or the other party or both get less than the full measure of what they want—need not be the rule. We discover that most often there is agreement and consensus on how to proceed.

We find that we develop the capacity to inspire and to be inspired by each other's thoughts and ideas. When we are invested in helping each other we ensure that we grow spiritually in ways that we cannot foresee. We have that "true" relationship that goes beyond the temporary sensations of passion or romance. We have something that is lasting and fulfilling, something that will carry us through eternity. When we look upon the face of our beloved, we see the friend who knows us best, our chosen life's companion, the spiritual partner whose needs we care for as much as our own. When we pray, we remember our love and ask for God's blessings and assistance.

Selected Prayers from Bahá'í Scripture

Glory be unto Thee, O my God! Verily, this Thy servant and this Thy maidservant have gathered under the shadow of Thy mercy and they are united through Thy favor and generosity. O Lord! Assist them in this Thy world and Thy kingdom and destine for them every good through Thy bounty and grace. O Lord! Confirm them in Thy servitude and assist them in Thy service. Suffer them to become the signs of Thy Name in Thy world and protect them through Thy bestowals which are inexhaustible in this world and the world to come. O Lord! They are supplicating the kingdom of Thy mercifulness and invoking the realm of Thy singleness. Verily, they are married in obedience to Thy command. Cause them to become the signs of harmony and unity until the end of time. Verily, Thou art the Omnipotent, the Omnipresent and the Almighty![12]

O my Lord, O my Lord! These two bright orbs are wedded in Thy love, conjoined in servitude to Thy Holy Threshold, united in ministering to Thy Cause. Make Thou this marriage to be as threading lights of Thine abounding grace, O my Lord, the All-Merciful, and luminous rays of Thy bestowals, O Thou the Beneficent, the Ever-Giving, that there may branch out from this great tree boughs that will grow green and flourishing through the gifts that rain down from Thy clouds of grace.

Verily, Thou art the Generous. Verily, Thou art the Almighty. Verily, Thou art the Compassionate, the All-Merciful.[13]

7

Raising Children Spiritually

*Among the greatest of all services that can possibly
be rendered by man to Almighty God is the
education and training of children.*
—'ABDU'L-BAHÁ

Human happiness is founded upon spiritual behavior.
—'ABDU'L-BAHÁ

Our destiny and success as a society rest largely upon the attitude we take toward the development and welfare of our children. Raising children is potentially one of the most challenging and rewarding experiences in life. While many will say child rearing is extremely difficult, most will also quickly point out that all of the associated challenges are well worth the effort, pain, frustration, and sacrifice they involve. This apparent contradiction suggests the depth and scope of the love that is present between parent and child. This chapter will look at the particular responsibilities that parents face as they strive to raise their children spiritually.

Parents are responsible for creating an environment within which their children can thrive and grow. To fulfill even the basic requirements for ensuring a child's physical sustenance and comfort can be a daunting task in itself. Yet parents are also enjoined to create favorable conditions for healthy intellectual and emotional growth so that their children will have the opportunity to reach their full potential as human beings. But the most important and far-reaching responsibility that parents have is to foster their children's spiritual development. Empowered with the right tools to progress spiritually, children will flourish and become happy, capable, loving adults who understand their purpose in life. Raising children spiritually is among the greatest services we can render in God's sight. To do so involves teaching them love and reverence for God, spiritual discipline and obedience, and a sense of morality and virtue. It also involves accustoming them to hardship and empowering them with the educational and spiritual tools they need to succeed in life. These are responsibilities that neither parents nor communities can ignore without serious consequences.

These responsibilities toward children are not unique to the parent-child relationship. Though primary responsibility for raising children belongs to the parents, responsibility for the education and nurturance of children also extends to the community. Parents cannot succeed in their efforts to nurture their children if the community in which they reside does not give them the tools and support they need, nor can they succeed if the community bombards their children with conflicting messages that undermine the parents' efforts. Our example and attitudes are constantly being watched and absorbed by our children, who spend virtually all of their waking hours observing and learning. What we do or fail to do as a community affects the future of our children and, as a result, the future of society.

Children are the most precious treasure a community can possess, for in them are the promise and guarantee of the future. They bear the seeds of the character of future society which is largely shaped by what the adults constituting the community do or fail to do with respect to children. They are a trust no community can neglect with impunity. An all-embracing love of children, the manner of treating them, the quality of the attention shown them, the spirit of adult behavior toward them—these are all among the vital aspects of the requisite attitude. Love demands discipline, the courage to accustom children to hardship, not to indulge their whims or leave them entirely to their own devices. An atmosphere needs to be maintained in which children feel that they belong to the community and share in its purpose.[1]

The first responsibility in raising children spiritually is to teach them love and reverence for God. This is the essential foundation for spiritual development. From the earliest age, children will benefit greatly from seeing their parents turning to God for spiritual sustenance and guidance. Teaching children to have a deep love and reverence for God ensures that they will want to act according to His will and not their own. The earlier the idea of turning to God is nurtured in children, the deeper and more natural that connection will be.

Bahá'í scripture points out the value of teaching children at the earliest age to love God and to remember Him:

From the very beginning, the children must receive divine education and must continually be reminded to remember their God. Let the love of God pervade their inmost being, commingled with their mother's milk.[2]

The parents must exert every effort to rear their offspring to be religious, for should the children not attain this greatest of adornments, they will not obey their parents, which in a certain sense means that they will not obey God. Indeed, such children will show no consideration to anyone, and will do exactly as they please.[3]

Let them strive by day and by night to establish within their children faith and certitude, the fear of God, . . . and all good qualities and traits.[4]

Parents are in a critical position to shape the spiritual development of their children. They should not ever underestimate their capacity to mold their children's moral character. For they exercise indispensable influence through the home environment they consciously create.[5]

When spiritual habits and values are introduced early and made a part of everyday life for children, a strong spiritual identity naturally develops. This requires a great deal of discipline and consistent effort on the part of parents and obedience on the part of children. Through these means the spiritual habits of prayer and regularly turning to God will take root.

It may be helpful here to say a few words about the concept of obedience. Obedience is a virtue, and its best companion is reason, not authoritarianism. In the same sense that blind faith is fraught with danger, so is our desire for blind obedience. When children rebel, it is often in response to an authoritarian approach. They need the constant opportunity to see that obedience is not an end in itself, but rather a means to guidance and understanding. To be effective, this must be a conclusion that our children arrive at for themselves because it is observably the way things work. Children need to be reared to understand that obedience has two parts: compliance and explanation. As children, we need to receive instruction and advice and then receive an explanation. The sequence is "Comply, then ask why," not the other way around. To question authority is to demand an explanation before obeying. When we do this, we end up only complying with those rules that we find agreeable. This is not obedience.

As parents we naturally want our children to be able to express themselves freely. However, freedom is often confused with license or licentiousness—the disregard of legal and moral restraints and the "freedom" to do whatever we want without being held responsible for our actions. There is not much freedom in having no rules or discipline. It may sound like a contradiction, but there is actually great freedom in strict obedience to laws. Traffic lights are a good example of this. When the light turns green, we cross the intersection, relying on other people to obey the law that requires them to stop on red. If everyone obeys this law, we are safe and free to not worry about what others will do. Children must not be left to assume that there are no rules or that there is no authority to which we must subjugate our will.

The image and likeness of God constitute the virtues of God, and man is intended to become the recipient of the effulgences of divine attributes. This is the essential foundation of all the divine religions, the reality itself, common to all.[6]

Developing the virtues of self-discipline and obedience are just two of the important ways we can nurture our children spiritually. As mentioned in chapter 1, cultivating all of the virtues of God is a sure path for spiritual growth and improvement. There is no better time to begin developing the virtues of God than in childhood. These virtues include but are not limited to:

Assertiveness	Confidence	Creativity
Caring	Consideration	Detachment
Cleanliness	Courage	Determination
Compassion	Courtesy	Enthusiasm

Excellence	Justice	Respect
Faithfulness	Kindness	Responsibility
Flexibility	Love	Reverence
Forgiveness	Loyalty	Self-Discipline
Friendliness	Mercy	Service
Generosity	Moderation	Steadfastness
Gentleness	Modesty	Tact
Helpfulness	Obedience	Thankfulness
Honesty	Orderliness	Tolerance
Honor	Patience	Trust
Humility	Peacefulness	Trustworthiness
Idealism	Purposefulness	Truthfulness
Joyfulness	Reliability	Unity

All of the world's religions make mention of these virtues. An education in the virtues can take shape in a variety of ways. Spiritual learning is not a process that is suited only to a classroom environment, for it is a learning experience that never stops. It is taught more by what we do than by what we say. Parents and other family members, who are the first teachers of their children, provide an example their children will readily follow, and there is much they can do to create learning opportunities. A formal education in a classroom setting with teachers as mentors and exemplars is yet another means by which children can learn and apply the many virtues of God in their own lives.

---

*While the children are yet in their infancy feed them
from the breast of heavenly grace, foster them in the*

cradle of all excellence, rear them in the embrace of bounty. Give them the advantage of every useful kind of knowledge. Let them share in every new and rare and wondrous craft and art. Bring them up to work and strive, and accustom them to hardship. Teach them to dedicate their lives to matters of great import, and inspire them to undertake studies that will benefit mankind.[7]

Another responsibility we face if we are trying to raise our children spiritually is to accustom them to hardship. This may be a novel and perhaps even shocking notion to many parents. The last thing we want for our children is to see them suffer or know sadness; it's painful for us to see our children suffer. Yet there is an undeniable wisdom to this principle, which has been touched upon in earlier chapters. Perhaps the wisest person is the one who has grown up with an appreciation for, and an understanding of, what it means to struggle in life. Having too many privileges without earning them or receiving too many things without having to work for them prevents a person from learning empathy and precludes the understanding that can be gained from making personal sacrifices.

For children, learning that not every demand is responded to favorably and that not every path is easily traversed is a valuable spiritual lesson. After all, growing up is itself a struggle. A good analogy that illustrates this principle can be seen in the infant who is trying to learn to sit up on her own. A father can lovingly help the baby to sit by propping her up with pillows or balancing her against his own body. When the father does this the baby is in fact "sitting up," but the necessary development is for the baby to learn and to develop the physical strength to do it herself. This is not a simple feat. It takes months of physical development, practice, and frustration before this skill—one that most physically capable adults take for granted—is mastered. Though there will inevitably be falls and mishaps along the way, and though it would be easier and less painful for the baby to give up and quit trying, the parents know that this is an important, if challenging, physical milestone. If the child gives up at this stage and is not willing to endure the frustration or put forth the effort to master the skill, her development is arrested and other important physical developmental milestones such as crawling, standing, walking, and so forth, will be nearly impossible to reach.

There is great value in realizing that some lessons are very hard to learn, some goals are not attainable, and suffering has its place. If children do not learn this, they will not be prepared for the unexpected, unfortunate, and unavoidable reality of tragedy and loss in their own lives. This will make it much more difficult for them to grow beyond their current spiritual condition to develop the virtues latent within their souls. Perhaps the hardest lesson for parents to learn is not to accommodate their children's every whim or fancy but to instill an appropriate sense of the need for, and value of, sacrifice and struggle in their lives. This notion has to be balanced with moderation, however, as the intent is not to force children to suffer unreasonably but to help them realize that disappointment and struggle are just normal, necessary parts of the process of spiritual growth and improvement.

It is incumbent upon the father and mother to train their children both in good conduct and the study of books; study, that is, to the degree required, so that no child, whether girl or boy, will remain illiterate.[8]

While we strive to assist our children's spiritual development, we cannot neglect another important area that affects their personal growth and prosperity: education. Education is an unquestioned necessity for the advancement of our greater society. The importance of creating a culture of learning for our children cannot be overemphasized. We need to see education as a progressive lifetime pursuit in which the expectation is to advance beyond the ability to read and write so that we can comprehend nuance and conceptual associations within the written word. Such a view sees education as a never-ending process, the goal of which is not merely to become literate but to become learned. This is something we can instill in our children by example. To render a good example is the responsibility of both parents; however, the mother is usually the first person the child bonds with, and she therefore has a greater influence over that learning process. Bahá'í scripture makes this very clear:

> The mother is the first teacher of the child. For children, at the beginning of life, are fresh and tender as a young twig, and can be trained in any fashion you desire. If you rear the child to be straight, he will grow straight, in perfect symmetry. It is clear that the mother is the first teacher and that it is she who establisheth the character and conduct of the child.[9]

O ye loving mothers, know ye that in God's sight, the best of all ways to worship Him is to educate the children and train them in all the perfections of humankind; and no nobler deed than this can be imagined.[10]

In fact, Bahá'í scripture indicates that in the matter of education, if parents are faced with having to choose between educating their sons or daughters, they are enjoined to educate their daughters first. This is because of the role that these future mothers will eventually play in their own children's education. Thus the emphasis is on ensuring that women are well educated and prepared to see to all of the requisite components of their children's proper emotional, physical, intellectual, and spiritual development. This principle does not contradict the Bahá'í teachings that all children should be educated and that fathers have an equally important role to play in providing for the children's education; it reinforces the value that is placed on the education of women. In a well-functioning community a family should be able to receive support for their children's education, for it is in the community's best interests to ensure that the educational needs of all children are met.

Education and training are recorded in the Book of God as obligatory and not voluntary. That is, it is enjoined upon the father and mother, as a duty, to strive with all effort to train the daughter and the son, to nurse them from the breast of knowledge and to rear them in the bosom of sciences and arts.[11]

Spiritual education is the process of developing virtues, those spiritual qualities that God has imbued within us. Social education requires the same development because the skills required to form and maintain healthy interpersonal relationships are all based on these same virtues. We must raise the level of our expectations continually upward and not teach our children to make peace with mediocrity by demonstrating our acceptance of it. We must teach by example, striving for excellence in everything we do. This does not mean that we try to exceed others but that we actualize our own potential and exceed ourselves.

Certainly, certainly, neglect not the education of the children. Rear them to be possessed of spiritual qualities, and be assured of the gifts and favours of the Lord.[12]

O Thou kind Lord! These lovely children are the handiwork of the fingers of Thy might and the wondrous signs of Thy greatness. O God! Protect these children, graciously assist them to be educated and enable them to render service to the world of humanity. O God! These children are pearls, cause them to be nurtured within the shell of Thy loving-kindness. Thou art the Bountiful, the All-Loving.[13]

Practical education involves not only the cultivation of mental and spiritual skills, but also hands-on, or manual, experience. This allows us to give form to the thoughts and ideas that come to us as inspiration. These manual skills are essential to our overall education because through them we learn to build and not destroy, to cherish and not break that which is beauteous in the world. For beauty to be valued, it must sometimes be shaped by hand and not just passively observed. It is a long-understood fact that we are less likely to devalue, deface, or vandalize that which we have designed, constructed, or decorated. Appreciation sometimes requires personal involvement. The attractiveness of a garden is enhanced when we have a hand in its planting and upkeep; art and music take on special meaning if we have developed the skills to produce or perform them ourselves. The following extract from Bahá'í scripture elaborates on the importance of applying what we know:

> High aims and pure motives, however laudable in themselves, will surely not suffice if unsupported by measures that are practicable and methods that are sound.[14]

These practical mental, physical, and spiritual components of education are all essential to the character development of children. Parents need to praise and sustain those parts of emerging character that are beneficial, identify and correct those that are not, and learn to tell the difference. It is important to begin shaping the process of character development from the very beginning, because the longer we delay the process, the more difficult it becomes. Every child is born in a state of purity, innocence, and nobility that can be built upon; however, without care and guidance, this purity and innocence is soon replaced with unruly attitudes and behaviors that take root and become increasingly difficult to eradicate with the passage of time.

The education and training of children is among the most meritorious acts of humankind and draweth down the grace and favor of the All-Merciful, for education is the indispensable foundation of all human excellence and alloweth man to work his way to the heights of abiding glory.[15]

Praying for and with our children is an integral part of spiritual parenting. Even from the child's first days in the womb, we need to speak of God in the presence of our children so that later in life believing in God and turning to Him for guidance will come naturally to them.

It is never too early for a child to establish a relationship with God, to memorize prayers, and get into the habit of saying them each day. In the beginning, children need their parents' assistance to read or recite prayers, but if this is done regularly and consistently, soon they learn to pray on their own without the prompting of others.

As children grow and mature they can continue to deepen this relationship with God through prayer. Even when they are adults we do not stop praying for their growth and well-being. The best gift we can give to our children is to raise them with the spiritual strength to one day raise a family of their own that worships God and is spiritually focused.

Selected Prayers from Bahá'í Scripture

Glorified art Thou, O Lord my God! I give Thee thanks inasmuch as Thou hast called me into being in Thy days, and infused into me Thy love and Thy knowledge. I beseech Thee, by Thy name whereby the goodly pearls of Thy wisdom and Thine utterance were brought forth out of the treasuries of the hearts of such of Thy servants as are nigh unto Thee, and through which the Day-Star of Thy name, the Compassionate, hath shed its radiance upon all that are in Thy heaven and on Thy earth, to supply me, by Thy grace and bounty, with Thy wondrous and hidden bounties.

These are the earliest days of my life, O my God, which Thou hast linked with Thine own days. Now that Thou hast conferred upon me so great an honor, withhold not from me the things Thou hast ordained for Thy chosen ones. I am, O my God, but a tiny seed which Thou hast sown in the soil of Thy love, and caused to spring forth by the hand of Thy bounty. This seed craveth, therefore, in its inmost being, for the waters of Thy mercy and the living fountain of Thy grace. Send down upon it, from the heaven of Thy loving-kindness, that which will enable it to flourish beneath Thy shadow and within the borders of Thy court. Thou art He Who watereth the hearts of all that have recognized Thee from Thy plenteous stream and the fountain of Thy living waters.

Praised be God, the Lord of the worlds.[16]

O Lord! Graciously assist this child to grow and be quickened in the meads of Thy tender affection. Thou art verily the Bestower, the Merciful, the Compassionate.[17]

O God, guide me, protect me, make of me a shining lamp and a brilliant star. Thou art the Mighty and the Powerful.[18]

O God! Educate these children. These children are the plants of Thine orchard, the flowers of Thy meadow, the roses of Thy garden. Let Thy rain fall upon them; let the Sun of Reality shine upon them with Thy love. Let Thy breeze refresh them in order that they may be trained, grow and develop, and appear in the utmost beauty.

Thou art the Giver. Thou art the Compassionate.[19]

O Lord! I am a child; enable me to grow beneath the shadow of Thy loving-kindness. I am a tender plant; cause me to be nurtured through the outpourings of the clouds of Thy bounty. I am a sapling of the garden of love; make me into a fruitful tree.

Thou art the Mighty and the Powerful, and Thou art the All-Loving, the All-Knowing, the All-Seeing.[20]

Part 3

Expanding the Circle of Unity

The utterance of God is a lamp, whose light is these words: Ye are the fruits of one tree, and the leaves of one branch. Deal ye one with another with the utmost love and harmony, with friendliness and fellowship. . . . So powerful is the light of unity that it can illuminate the whole earth.
—BAHÁ'U'LLÁH

Unity is necessary to existence.
—'ABDU'L-BAHÁ

As the circle of unity expands to include others beyond our spouses, families, relatives, and neighbors, a new appreciation for unity emerges. The same sense of belonging we enjoy locally can be applied globally. We live in a wonderful age in which we can make acquaintances and friends with people virtually anywhere on the planet. We can now do this in person through travel or without leaving our own homes. The Internet, various forms of telecommunication, and especially television offer pathways that can take us almost anywhere we want to go. We can reach out and interact with people nearly anywhere in the world. There are great benefits in doing this, and each interaction changes who we are.

Perhaps the most beneficial consequence of this interaction is the possibility of successfully dealing with some of our longstanding social problems such as racism, nationalism, sexism, and economic disparity. These kinds of problems were largely unaddressed and unresolved when we lived in relative isolation from each other and when travel was difficult and communication often impossible. However, circumstances have changed, enabling us to see more and more how inextricably our lives are connected. We have come to realize, whether willingly or not, that despite our diverse ways we all belong to one world and share a common destiny. We have come to understand that diversity is more than watching a documentary about people from other countries—it is people coming together and exchanging and appreciating each others' beliefs, ideas, values, and customs. We celebrate the extent of diversity in the world when we learn to compare our similarities rather than simply contrast our differences. As we do this we discover that we have a lot to offer each other. Increasingly we are discovering new ways to better share our talents and serve the needs of the world community to which we all belong.

Geographical isolation and social segregation have shaped many of the beliefs we have come to take for granted—assumptions that were rarely discussed or challenged until recently. We have come to see that many of our values and cultural standards of behavior are based on some very erroneous and outmoded beliefs. The most common of these is superiority. The assumption that one person is somehow superior to another has contributed to some of our greatest social ills. It is this presumption that drives racism, nationalism, sexism, poverty, and many other social ills.

The chapters that follow focus on spiritual solutions to these lingering social problems. Bahá'í scripture provides clear insights in this regard. It reveals that enduring change comes from within and that the best place to start to change the world for the better is within our own hearts. The world can be changed one heart at a time, and this is what draws us closer to each other. We are all equal in this.

The key to unity is the personal discovery of the oneness of humanity. When we truly embrace our diversity, our appreciation for each other turns to love, and that love transforms us as people, affecting the quality of our families and communities. This widening circle of love and appreciation grows until it encompasses the earth. We become world citizens without relinquishing our local, regional, or national affiliations. By being more than the sum of our affiliations to a particular place, we acquire the highest layer of affiliation, an alliance to the well-being of the entire planet. In the pages ahead we will also see that one of the most significant ways to achieve unity is by being of service to each other. Social interaction and relationships are fundamental to unity, and service to others is one of the requirements for establishing peace not only within ourselves but also in our communities and beyond.

8

Uniting with Each Other and the World

Be thou a summoner to love, and be thou kind to all the human race. Love thou the children of men and share in their sorrows. Be thou of those who foster peace. Offer thy friendship, be worthy of trust. Be thou a balm to every sore, be thou a medicine for every ill. Bind thou the souls together.
—ʻABDUʼL-BAHÁ

A world at peace has long been the dream of humankind. The yearning for a planet that is not only without warfare and violence but also united as one family is universal. Though realization of this dream is no easy task, the potential rewards of bringing people together are great. As always, the starting place is found within the individual. As we focus on our own personal understandings of what it takes to create peace within ourselves, we begin to establish peace within our families. Family unity naturally spills over to become the building block of peace within our nations, which will eventually help create a peaceful world. To begin this process, we must examine any barriers that prevent unity. Two in particular are related to how we view strangers.

The first barrier is the way we view the world in general. If we believe that the world is composed of individual nations and not of individual people, this creates a mentality that tends to perceive frontiers, clear lines along borders, and boundaries beyond which lie foreigners and aliens. Bahá'u'lláh has provided a new perspective to overcome this:

The earth is but one country, and mankind its citizens.[1]

Before our initial reaches into space in the middle of the twentieth century, our view of the world was often consistent with the image of a classroom globe: a sphere composed of different-colored countries. That first photograph of the blue-green planet Earth that was taken from space helped change our view of the world. From space, Earth does not appear divided; there are no countries, no borders, no foreigners. Earth is the home and dwelling place of all people.

This span of earth is but one homeland and one habitation.[2]

He Who is your Lord, the All-Merciful, cherisheth in His heart the desire of beholding the entire human race as one soul and one body.[3]

The second barrier is the way we view others in general. We often see people not as unique individuals, but rather as representatives of a particular group. This barrier is harder to overcome because unity cannot be established between groups of people until it is achieved among individuals. There is a reason for this. The way we group people is very arbitrary and simplistic. Race, nationality, and ethnicity are often tacitly defined by a particular set of traits, the presumed attributes of a group. Coming up with a name for a group of people does not make the grouping real, and assigning someone to a group isn't just a superficial appraisal of who that person is—it makes that person archetypal of the group. The individual becomes invisible to the extent that only the presumed attributes are seen. This perspective is the root of racial profiling, and it is not just a problem among law enforcement professionals. It is the barrier of prejudice that all of us must work to overcome.

Unless ye must,
Bruise not the serpent in the dust,
How much less wound a man.
And if ye can,
No ant should ye alarm,
Much less a brother harm.[4]

Our views of others are based on deep-seated beliefs that we may rarely examine. They remain unchallenged and, admit it or not, we often assume that stereotypes are real—that "Jewishness," "African-Americanness," "Hispanicness," and "Whiteness" are real. These become identities based upon our view of outward appearances, behaviors, and myths. They do not describe individual people, only the presumed distinction of groups, and everyday language usage tends to legitimatize them as meaningful expressions of identity. But they do not, in reality, define who we are, or who other people are.

But people want some form of identity. People have come to understand that the question "What are you?" cannot be answered definitively with a single word. Answering simply "American" does not convey much information if both people are Americans. Both parties already know that all Americans are different. Social identity is never that simple. We recognize that identifying ourselves as one thing does not exclude our being many other things as well. In answer to the question "What are you?" a person can say that he is "an Oregonian." This does not necessarily mean that he was born and raised in Oregon. He may well have been born in California and lived in a dozen states before moving to Oregon. It could be a statement of where he currently resides. Depending on the context of the question, the appropriate answer could be any number of diminishing geographical identities.

No matter where we live, there are national, regional, and local designations that we employ to see ourselves as different or special. In truth, our social identity is always many-layered. Some of the layers are defined not solely by who we are but by our ancestry. Deep-rooted beliefs about social class, caste, nationality, citizenship, ethnicity, origin, heritage, and ancestry are often used to draw lines of distinction and discrimination between people. These erroneous beliefs form the rationale of privilege and social superiority. But Bahá'í scripture reminds us of our essential oneness:

Know ye not why We created you all from the same dust? That no one should exalt himself over the other. Ponder at all times in your hearts how ye were created. Since We have created you all from one same substance it is incumbent on you to be even as one soul, to walk with the same feet, eat with the same mouth and dwell in the same land, that from your inmost being, by your deeds and actions, the signs of oneness and the essence of detachment may be made manifest.[5]

Each of our deep-rooted, erroneous beliefs needs to be replaced with a new understanding of oneness. Oneness is the acknowledgment, above all else, that we are all fellow humans and that we are equal in the sight of our Creator.

God, the Almighty, has created all mankind from the dust of earth. He has fashioned them all from the same elements; they are descended from the same race and live upon the same globe. He has created them to dwell beneath the one heaven. . . . He has made no distinction in mercies and graces among His children.[6]

O ye beloved of the Lord! This day is the day of union, the day of the ingathering of all mankind.[7]

God has willed that love should be a vital force in the world.[8]

We need to embrace this reality and act accordingly, to put aside prejudicial attitudes and beliefs and live as one people on one planet. The result of acknowledging our inherent oneness is unity, and Bahá'u'lláh describes the potent effect of its realization:

So powerful is the light of unity that it can illuminate the whole earth.[9]

We must endeavor to avoid becoming so preoccupied with our pride of place, our regionalism, or our nationalism as to cause us to forget that beyond the simple geography of political borders, we all find ourselves dwelling on the same planet.

It is not for him to pride himself who loveth his own country, but rather for him who loveth the whole world.[10]

Ye are the fruits of one tree and the leaves of one branch; be ye compassionate and kind to all the human race.[11]

As seen from space, the earth is clearly one place, a single homeland to all humanity, and there are no national boundary lines. Nevertheless, the rivalries and wars of the past have made certain groups of people seem like strangers to each other.

Shut your eyes to estrangement, then fix your gaze upon unity. Cleave tenaciously unto that which will lead to the well-being and tranquillity of all mankind.[12]

Strive to attain a station of absolute love one toward another. By the absence of love, enmity increases. By the exercise of love, love strengthens and enmities dwindle away.[13]

The word of God, with its "collective wisdom, absolute knowledge and eternal truth,"[14] has always endeavored to raise our vision and understanding to see beyond our immediate environment. Only its penetrating influence, Bahá'í scripture asserts, can unite humanity:

Naught but the celestial potency of the Word of God . . . is capable of harmonizing the divergent thoughts, sentiments, ideas and convictions of the children of men.[15]

Praise be to God, today the splendor of the Word of God hath illumined every horizon, and from all sects, races, tribes, nations, and communities souls have come together in the light of the Word, assembled, united and agreed in perfect harmony. . . . Verily, this is from the penetrative power of the Word of God!

If all the forces of the universe were to combine they would not be able thus to gather a single assemblage so imbued with the sentiments of love, affection, attraction and enkindlement as to unite the members of different races and to raise up from the heart of the world a voice that shall dispel war and strife, uproot dissension and disputation, usher in the era of universal peace and establish unity and concord amongst men.[16]

As with the whole, so with the parts; whether a flower or a human body, when the attracting principle is withdrawn from it, the flower or the man dies. It is therefore clear that attraction, harmony, unity and Love, are the cause of life, whereas repulsion, discord, hatred and separation bring death.[17]

The Bahá'í teachings stress that harmony, love, attraction, and union are the life of the world of humanity, while repulsion, discord, hatred, and separation are things which lead to its death.

Love is the fundamental principle of God's purpose for man, and He has commanded us to love each other even as He loves us.[18]

Love and good faith must so dominate the human heart that men will regard the stranger as a familiar friend,

*the malefactor as one of their own, the alien even as a
loved one, the enemy as a companion dear and close.*[19]

Unity requires us to keep in mind that we are
three things at the same time: different, equal,
and together. These cannot be dealt with separately; we cannot discuss diversity, equality, or
oneness in isolation. They are interconnected
components. Without the component of equality, social diversity stratifies into social hierar-
chy. Cultural and social differences imply neither inferiority nor superiority. There are no first-
class or second-class citizens in the sight of God.
Without the component of oneness, without the
basic realization that we share a common fate
and that we are all together here on the same
planet, we develop destructive systems such as
segregation and apartheid that serve the interests of the few at the expense of the many. Such
systems falsely propose that people can be separate but equal. In reality, these systems have
repeatedly shown that they never promote equality or perpetuate mutual love. Such systems can
only be maintained through tyranny, and their
results are hatred and violence.

---

*How long will humanity persist in its waywardness?
How long will injustice continue? How long is chaos
and confusion to reign amongst men? How long will
discord agitate the face of society? . . . The winds of*

despair are, alas, blowing from every direction, and the strife that divideth and afflicteth the human race is daily increasing.[20]

Beware lest ye harm any soul, or make any heart to sorrow; lest ye wound any man with your words, be he known to you or a stranger, be he friend or foe. Pray ye for all; ask ye that all be blessed, all be forgiven. . . . Beware, beware, lest ye offend the feelings of another, even though he be an evil-doer, and he wish you ill.[21]

Without a new perspective, one that enables us to see each other as God sees us, we can never establish unity in the world. We need a spiritual perspective:

You must manifest complete love and affection toward all mankind. . . . Know that God is compassionate toward all; therefore, love all from the depths of your hearts, . . . be filled with love for every race, and be kind toward the people of all nationalities.[22]

The use of prayer and reliance on the word of God are the most powerful means by which we can turn to God to help us unite with each other. Nothing short of that will help us build true, lasting unity in the world. It requires spiritual fortitude, and the word of God is the greatest source of strength that we can access.

Selected Prayers from Bahá'í Scripture

O my God! O my God! Unite the hearts of Thy servants, and reveal to them Thy great purpose. May they follow Thy commandments and abide in Thy law. Help them, O God, in their endeavor, and grant them strength to serve Thee. O God! Leave them not to themselves, but guide their steps by the light of Thy knowledge, and cheer their hearts by Thy love. Verily, Thou art their Helper and their Lord.[23]

O Thou kind Lord! Thou hast created all humanity from the same stock. Thou hast decreed that all shall belong to the same household. In Thy Holy Presence they are all Thy servants, and all mankind are sheltered beneath Thy Tabernacle; all have gathered together at Thy Table of Bounty; all are illumined through the light of Thy Providence. O God! Thou art kind to all, Thou hast provided for all, dost shelter all, conferrest life upon all. Thou hast endowed each and all with talents and faculties, and all are submerged in the Ocean of Thy Mercy.

O Thou kind Lord! Unite all. Let the religions agree and make the nations one, so that they may see each other as one family and the whole earth as one home. May they all live together in perfect harmony.

O God! Raise aloft the banner of the oneness of mankind.

O God! Establish the Most Great Peace. Cement Thou, O God, the hearts together.

O Thou kind Father, God! Gladden our hearts through the fragrance of Thy love. Brighten our eyes through the Light of Thy Guidance. Delight our ears with the melody of Thy Word, and shelter us all in the Stronghold of Thy Providence.

Thou art the Mighty and Powerful, Thou art the Forgiving and Thou art the One Who overlooketh the shortcomings of all mankind.[24]

O God, my God! Aid Thou Thy trusted servants to have loving and tender hearts. Help them to spread, amongst all the nations of the earth, the light of guidance that cometh from the Company on high. Verily, Thou art the Strong, the Powerful, the Mighty, the All-Subduing, the Ever-Giving. Verily, Thou art the Generous, the Gentle, the Tender, the Most Bountiful.[25]

9

Working toward Racial Unity

O ye beloved of God! Know ye, verily, that the happiness of mankind lieth in the unity and the harmony of the human race, and that spiritual and material developments are conditioned upon love and amity among all men.
—'ABDU'L-BAHÁ

As we look beyond our own spiritual well-being and that of our immediate family, we consider the community and the world beyond us. Uniting with others requires new kinds of behavior and new levels of understanding that we have never reached before. If we acknowledge the need for nations to coexist peacefully, we must also eliminate those unhealthy racial divides that have long plagued humanity, for racial unity is a crucial prerequisite to the progress and health of all humanity. Racial unity brings the promise of untold possibilities and hopes fulfilled. It means the end to age-old misguided notions of superiority and inferiority and the beginning of a new way of life for all civilization. Realizing racial unity ensures the true happiness and progress of humanity and guarantees a world where spiritual qualities, not physical attributes, are the measure of one's character and chances in life. Racial unity is not a result of political measures to enact laws, but is the result of a spiritual transformation. It is something we are all capable of achieving if we will only take the first step. Racial unity is not sameness, nor is it the enforcement of the will of one ethnicity over another. It is the celebration of our common humanity as we work together to build strong communities, treating each other as members of one family. This chapter examines some of the challenges that have to be overcome to achieve this noble destiny and offers hope that it can, in fact, be attained.

The notion that people can and should be classified by race, and thereby subjected to either prejudicial or preferential treatment, is America's most challenging issue. It is the cause of untold daily injustices and pervades every area of social interaction in the United States. It has been institutionalized in the form of birth certificates, census forms, and job applications requiring people to categorize themselves by the very tenuous attribute of race. In the vernacular, we often employ color names to indicate races which, upon reflection, describe no human pigmentation. Upon examination, there is no one on this planet who is truly pure white, black, red, or yellow. Still, the use of these terms to describe people persists. This is strange because if we look closely at ourselves, each of us has a variety of colors over our bodies, not just one color. Standing side by side, if we look for colors rather than races, we can easily see that collectively humankind is a continuum of complex hues. There are no groups of colors and certainly no clear boundaries separating colors.

I pray that you attain to such a degree of good character and behavior that the names of black and white shall vanish. All shall be called human.[1]

Why, then, do we group people by race? The answer is that we have learned to see something that is not really there. It is generally accepted by modern-day anthropologists that all human beings share common ancestral roots that originated on the African continent millions of years ago. When humans began migrating to other parts of the world where the climate and environment were different, the process of natural selection ensured the survival and reproductive success of those who were best suited to their environment. This led to the perpetuation of whatever genetic qualities were best suited to each particular environment. The physical variations we see today in people from different parts of the world are, therefore, all variations within a single species, the human species. There is only one race, the human race, and whatever terms we may use to categorize each other are merely the result of many generations of misguided notions about what superficial physical differences mean.

A critic may object, saying that peoples, races, tribes and communities of the world are of different and varied customs, habits, tastes, character, inclinations and ideas, that opinions and thoughts are contrary to one another, and how, therefore, is it possible for real unity to be revealed and perfect accord among human souls to exist?

In answer we say that differences are of two kinds. One is the cause of annihilation and is like the an-

> *tipathy existing among warring nations and conflict-*
> *ing tribes who seek each other's destruction, uprooting*
> *one another's families, depriving one another of rest*
> *and comfort and unleashing carnage. The other kind*
> *which is a token of diversity is the essence of perfection*
> *and the cause of the appearance of the bestowals of the*
> *Most Glorious Lord.*[2]

We rarely stop to examine the meanings of the words we use to categorize one another or ask why terms like "Caucasian" are seen as somehow more correct than "White." Unfortunately, when terms referring to colors are replaced with terms referring to supposed geographical origins, one set of false premises simply replaces another. In fact, despite the findings of the national census, very few of us can trace our ancestry to people who emigrated to these shores from the Caucasus Mountains of western Asia.

While we are considering words that describe particular groups of people, it is important to realize that there can be legitimate historical and social reasons for doing so. For example, the term "African American" is not just a racial designation. It carries with it a legitimate and profound sense of heritage, a shared common social and cultural experience that spans a remembered and oftentimes painful past and a significant number of generations. It is a line of heritage that has seen many terms applied to it, some positive and some extremely hurtful: "Negro," "Colored," "Black," "Afro-American," "African American." The fact that these designations have changed over time in compliance with an ever-shifting sense of political correctness should suggest to us not only that the terms are arbitrary but also that the concept of race itself and the divisions that it creates are arbitrary as well.

To bring the white and the black together is considered impossible and unfeasible, but the breaths of the Holy Spirit will bring about this union.

. . . the enmity and hatred which exist between the white and the black races is very dangerous and there is no doubt that it will end in bloodshed unless the influence of the Word of God, the breaths of the Holy Spirit and the teachings of Bahá'u'lláh are diffused amongst them and harmony is established between the two races.[3]

Rather than perpetuating the idea of race, we need to encourage our children and each other to discern and celebrate the diversity of each one's heritage. Our heritages are the rich soil from which we sprang, and, together with the fruit of our own lives, they help to define who we are. Heritage is inclusive of social and cultural realities and recognizes that we are very complex beings who can trace many lines of ancestors from many backgrounds. Acknowledging each other's heritage and diversity also legitimizes our own because we are reminded that, as human beings, we all share a common ancestry.

God has endowed man with virtues, powers and ideal faculties of which nature is entirely bereft and by which man is elevated, distinguished and superior. We must thank God for these bestowals, for these powers He has given us, for this crown He has placed upon our heads.

How shall we utilize these gifts and expend these bounties? By directing our efforts toward the unification of the human race. We must use these powers in establishing the oneness of the world of humanity, appreciate these virtues by accomplishing the unity of whites and blacks, devote this divine intelligence to the perfecting of amity and accord among all branches of the human family so that under the protection and providence of God the East and West may hold each other's hands and become as lovers. Then will mankind be as one nation, one race and kind—as waves of one ocean.[4]

The belief in different races produces a strange kind of social blindness that tends to negate the reality of who we really are and render unseen the beauty of our individual characters.

The wonder and complexity of our inner spiritual being also goes unnoticed under the myopia of racism. Unlike beauty, racism is a sty in the eye of the beholder. It impedes our vision of each other to the point where we cannot see the beauty. But there is hope for us. As long as children, who are born without the concept of race, are raised by parents who strive day by day to cure themselves of the affliction of racial prejudice, there is hope that we will eventually inhabit the world Dr. Martin Luther King, Jr., spoke of, a world in which people are judged not by the color of their skin but by the content of their character. This is no longer just a dream. Today there are places in the world where this is already happening. Bahá'ís throughout the world are striving to live this way.

When the racial elements of the American nation unite in actual fellowship and accord, the lights of the oneness of humanity will shine, the day of eternal glory and bliss will dawn, the spirit of God encompass, and the divine favors descend. Under the leadership and training of God, the real Shepherd, all will be protected and preserved. He will lead them in green pastures of happiness and sustenance, and they will attain to the real goal of existence. This is the blessing and benefit of unity; this is the outcome of love.[5]

For more than one hundred years Bahá'ís everywhere have been endeavoring to live according to God's message of unity and oneness for the world. The following words of Bahá'u'lláh encapsulate God's will for humanity in this regard:

> Verily, the words which have descended from the heaven of the Will of God are the source of unity and harmony for the world. Close your eyes to racial differences, and welcome all with the light of oneness.[6]

Since the beginning of the twentieth century, Bahá'ís in America have been helping to turn racial avoidance and antipathy into cooperation and amity.

If you meet those of a different race and color from yourself, do not mistrust them, and withdraw yourself into your shell of conventionality, but rather be glad and show them kindness.[7]

It is possible to change the way we view the world so that we perceive beauty and are not blinded by hatred and prejudice. Bahá'í scripture describes the true beauty in store for us when we see those things that distinguish human beings as assets and not as hindrances:

> In the clustered jewels of the races may the blacks be as sapphires and rubies and the

whites as diamonds and pearls. The composite beauty of humanity will be witnessed in their unity and blending. How glorious the spectacle of real unity among mankind! How conducive to peace, confidence and happiness if races and nations were united in fellowship and accord! The Prophets of God were sent into the world upon this mission of unity and agreement: that these long-separated sheep might flock together.[8]

Because we are essentially spiritual beings, when we depart from this physical world to the life hereafter, we leave behind all the aspects of this physical existence. The body does not accompany the soul on its hereafter. There are no races in heaven, only souls. The soul is the most important part of our being.

There are no whites and blacks before God. All colors are one, and that is the color of servitude to God.[9]

If the heart is pure, white or black or any color makes no difference. God does not look at colors; He looks at the hearts.[10]

When we realize that one's external appearance is secondary to one's inner spiritual being, we are well on the way toward abolishing estrangement and conflict. There is little doubt that the only way to achieve this is through spiritual means. The Bahá'í teachings clearly point out that by working toward racial unity we are rendering a great service to humanity.

Colors are nonessential characteristics, but the realities of men are essential. When there is unity of the essence, what power hath the ephemeral? When the light of reality is shining, what power hath the darkness of the unreal? If it be possible, gather together these two races—black and white—into one Assembly, and create such a love in the hearts that they shall not only unite, but blend into one reality. Know thou of a certainty that as a result differences and disputes between black and white will be totally abolished. By the Will of God, may it be so! This is a most great service to humanity.[11]

Turning to God in these matters, especially in prayer, will help us achieve a spiritual perspective. We can pray that we break down those barriers that keep us apart. We can pray to unite with each other and to improve our own lives, the lives of our children, and the lives of those around us.

Selected Prayers from Bahá'í Scripture

Is there any Remover of difficulties save God? Say: Praised be God! He is God! All are His servants, and all abide by His bidding![12]

Make firm our steps, O Lord, in Thy path and strengthen Thou our hearts in Thine obedience. Turn our faces toward the beauty of Thy oneness, and gladden our bosoms with the signs of Thy divine unity. Adorn our bodies with the robe of Thy bounty, and remove from our eyes the veil of sinfulness, and give us the chalice of Thy grace; that the essence of all beings may sing Thy praise before the vision of Thy grandeur. Reveal then Thyself, O Lord, by Thy merciful utterance and the mystery of Thy divine being, that the holy ecstasy of prayer may fill our souls—a prayer that shall rise above words and letters and transcend the murmur of syllables and sounds—that all things may be merged into nothingness before the revelation of Thy splendor.

Lord! These are servants that have remained fast and firm in Thy Covenant and Thy Testament, that have held fast unto the cord of constancy in Thy Cause and clung unto the hem of the robe of Thy grandeur. Assist them, O Lord, with Thy grace, confirm them with Thy power and strengthen their loins in obedience to Thee.

Thou art the Pardoner, the Gracious.[13]

10

Bringing about Gender Equality

Know thou . . . that . . . women are accounted the same as men, and God hath created all humankind in His own image, and after His own likeness. That is, men and women alike are the revealers of His names and attributes, and from the spiritual viewpoint there is no difference between them.
—'ABDU'L-BAHÁ

Whether we are a brother or sister, a mother or father, a husband or wife, we are touched by the need for equality and understanding across gender lines. There is no greater joy than realizing one's full potential as a human being, regardless of gender. Today, due to the advances in education and technology that our society now enjoys, once-traditional male or female roles are quickly changing and evolving. In fact, from family to family and from person to person, the concept of what those roles are is rarely identical. In many parts of the world today women enjoy greater opportunities than ever before, but there is still a lot of work to be done before we can truly say we have achieved equality.

It is erroneous to believe that the issue of gender equality is strictly a women's issue. Men, too, need opportunities to grow beyond traditional roles and to overcome the challenge of sexism, which hampers everyone's development. The Bahá'í Faith teaches that women and men can only achieve their full potential when both are given equal opportunities to grow and develop. In fact, as mentioned in chapter 7, the Bahá'í teachings indicate that if parents cannot afford to educate both their sons and daughters, preference should be given to their daughters. This does not imply that women are more important than men, but it does indicate the need to support them in their crucial role as the first educators of society. It is especially important for the daughter to be educated because she will later be the first educator of her own children and will have a profound influence on their character. She must be equipped with the means to teach them how to live, learn, and worship. To hold one gender back necessarily holds the other back as well. In the eyes of God, the Bahá'í teachings proclaim, there is no superior or inferior gender; God judges a soul on its qualities and character alone, not according to its gender. In this day and age both women and men are called to overcome the challenges of sexism to establish the reality of gender equality and harmony.

Uniting the two largest groups of people in the world into a harmoniously blended coexistence requires at least three crucial things to happen: the systematic elimination of gender prejudice, discernable progress toward the establishment of justice in the world, and the establishment of equality between women and men. Even though these goals are not easily accomplished, they can be achieved through both personal and unified efforts, and they are certainly within humanity's grasp.

The diversity in the human family should be the cause of love and harmony, as it is in music where many different notes blend together in the making of a perfect chord.[1]

For the individual, the process of replacing ignorance with understanding, tolerance, respect, and appreciation for the other gender is linked to changing the damaging attitudes that prevent both sexes from recognizing the advantages inherent in equality. For most of us this process is a difficult, lifelong pursuit. Fortunately our perspectives can be reshaped and corrected when we understand how God sees the issue of gender. Bahá'í scripture affirms that "Women and men have been and will always be equal in the sight of God. The Dawning-Place of the Light of God sheddeth its radiance upon all with the same effulgence."[2]

For the human race as a whole, and for men in particular, overcoming any sense of gender superiority is an ongoing process that requires patience and sustained effort. True and lasting progress is not going to be won through violent confrontations, power struggles, or political legislation, but rather through self-evaluation and a process of evolution that changes the root values by which we live and interact. Personal accountability and measured change are the fundamental processes that produce great and enduring civilizations, for they ensure the ability to adjust and survive in changing conditions and circumstances.

It is natural to feel impatient when we are hoping for improvements in the move toward gender equality. If we have seen injustice with our own eyes, we want changes to happen now, in our own lifetime. We are willing to struggle for our rights, and we want to enjoy the benefits of our personal labors. Unfortunately, progress and lasting change can usually only be seen and adequately evaluated in retrospect. When we look back on the history of the past millennium, it is easy to see that it has been dominated by wars fought because of national, racial, ideological, and religious intolerance. These wars have been highly visible and are thoroughly documented in history books. At the same time, there have been other less acknowledged and less documented struggles. The struggle for gender equality is one of these. In the lives of many women—and, consequently, in the lives of their loved ones—it has been as great a conflict as any of the world wars, even though it has been far less widely reported and studied.

If racism is racial prejudice, then sexism is gender prejudice, for it is based on the same erroneous premises which assert that some of us are superior to others. These beliefs and attitudes are manifest in behavior that segregates us by gender and discriminates in every area of human endeavor. It is a problem everywhere, and no nation is immune from this social ailment.

It has been objected by some that woman is not equally capable with man and that she is deficient by creation. This is pure imagination. The difference in

> *capability between man and woman is due entirely to*
> *opportunity and education.*[3]

Simplistic and sweeping generalities about gender are not only inaccurate and inadequate, they also prevent us from seeing the commonalities shared by both genders. Phrases such as "the opposite sex" are loaded with implications. If we see the genders as opposites, then whatever we see as characteristics of the other gender must be, by implication, the antithesis of what we are. While there are undeniable differences between the sexes, Bahá'í scripture explains that those differences that do exist between the sexes should be seen as complementary and beneficial:

> The world of humanity has two wings—one is women and the other men. Not until both wings are equally developed can the bird fly. Should one wing remain weak, flight is impossible. Not until the world of women becomes equal to the world of men in the acquisition of virtues and perfections, can success and prosperity be attained as they ought to be.[4]

According to Bahá'í teachings, all women and men are exhorted to engage in an occupation that will benefit themselves and others; it is the responsibility of individuals to know their true selves and abilities and to follow their God-given path in life. When true equality between women and men becomes a reality, society will not only support both genders in the pursuit of whatever occupation they are best suited for, but it will value all occupations, regardless of whether they be in the home or workplace. An occupation's value should not be based on what it pays or how much power it provides, but on what it contributes to society. When considered from this perspective, important roles such as motherhood are elevated. In fact, Bahá'í scripture points out that raising children is among the noblest deeds any person can perform. How a woman elects to fulfill her role as a mother is largely up to her and the particular needs of her family. The important principle here is that women and men are meant to fulfill their God-given capacities in this lifetime; how they choose to do so is a personal choice that should receive the loving support of the community.

Let us hope that we will come to see that the purpose of having wings is to fly. To achieve this, the present inertia of gender inequality and prejudice must be overcome so that a condition of healthy interdependence and cooperation can be established. For this metaphorical bird of humanity to fly, both wings—male and female— must be equally strong, and each must work in complete harmony with the other. For real birds, getting off the ground is the hardest part of flying, and the same is true for us. Once we are airborne there is little we can't do. We will become what we were designed to become: a lofty creation that can soar to heights that were unimaginable and unattainable while we were earthbound.

In the meantime, we must continue to prepare for flight. As society matures it will become easier to see that all of us participate in two kinds of activities: The first kind are those endeavors that come to fruition within the span of our own lives; the second kind are those for which we sow seeds now, realizing that they will only come to fruition for posterity, long after we are gone.

Through the effulgent rays of divine illumination the capacity of woman has become so awakened and manifest in this age that equality of man and woman is an established fact.[5]

Equality will be seen as more than a goal, for it will be recognized as the means to greater achievements for all. To make both wings equal is not the ultimate goal—the real goal is to fly, to raise humanity above its previous limitations. Furthermore, equality does not imply sameness;

it means ensuring that every individual is free to excel and to develop as his or her God-given talents warrant.

Equality between men and women is conducive to the abolition of warfare for the reason that women will never be willing to sanction it. Mothers will not give their sons as sacrifices upon the battlefield after twenty years of anxiety and loving devotion in rearing them from infancy, no matter what cause they are called upon to defend. There is no doubt that when women obtain equality of rights, war will entirely cease among mankind.[6]

For men, warfare on the battlefield has always been seen as a way to solve big problems. The rationale behind this method of problem solving is the belief that disputes can be solved by mustering a superior force and winning a physical contest. However, the physical contest rarely addresses the underlying issues that gave rise to the conflict, and some problems have an enormous inertia that does not allow them to be solved quickly. If something has been moving in one direction for a thousand years, for example, it stands to reason that its direction cannot be changed overnight. Such problems require the cooperation of generations of people who are working to improve a shared condition.

Let it be known . . . that until woman and man recognize and realize equality, social and political progress here or anywhere will not be possible. For the world of humanity consists of two parts or members: one is woman; the other is man. Until these two members are equal in strength, the oneness of humanity cannot be established, and the happiness and felicity of mankind will not be a reality.[7]

Often the goal of efforts to achieve equal rights is to remove the barriers that keep the oppressed from attaining equality. Yet there is another important goal, which is to free the oppressor. When one person maneuvers to keep another from advancing, energy and resources that could be spent more productively on something else are expended on keeping the other person down. When we hold someone down, we are not that far above them. To keep them there, we have to stay with them. As long as men do this to women, they cannot advance freely either.

Women have equal rights with men upon earth; in religion and society they are a very important element. As long as women are prevented from attaining their highest possibilities, so long will men be unable to achieve the greatness which might be theirs.[8]

Men should feel that the struggle for gender equality is also their struggle. It is not enough that women be seen as equal to men: Both genders should be seen as equal to something higher, something more human than the existing male or female ideals. True advancement for both women and men implies the creation of a new and as yet unrealized ideal in human achievement. Men must take an active role in ensuring that women are guaranteed freedom from oppression; they must work to overcome the sexual prejudice that they may harbor in their hearts; and they need to come to the realization that no true progress will ever take place until they grasp the truth that "gender equality" is not just a woman's issue—it is a human issue. By the same token, women must recognize their own internalized oppression and forgive past injustices; they must educate themselves and strive to realize their full human potential.

We ourselves may never live to see the establishment of a society based upon these values. However, what we do now will lay the groundwork for what the sons and daughters of the future will experience.

Together, male and female are greater than one or the other can ever be separately. Turning to God in prayer can be of great assistance in overcoming gender prejudice if we ask Him to help us look deep within ourselves to solve our problems. This will give us the spiritual fortitude to overcome age-old problems and progress toward a new future in which both women and men will realize their true capacities.

Selected Prayers from Bahá'í Scripture

Magnified be Thy name, O Lord my God! Behold Thou mine eye expectant to gaze on the wonders of Thy mercy, and mine ear longing to hearken unto Thy sweet melodies, and my heart yearning for the living waters of Thy knowledge. Thou seest Thy handmaiden, O my God, standing before the habitation of Thy mercy, and calling upon Thee by Thy name which Thou hast chosen above all other names and set up over all that are in heaven and on earth. Send down upon her the breaths of Thy mercy, that she may be carried away wholly from herself, and be drawn entirely towards the seat which, resplendent with the glory of Thy face, sheddeth afar the radiance of Thy sovereignty, and is established as Thy throne. Potent art Thou to do what Thou willest. No God is there beside Thee, the All-Glorious, the Most Bountiful.

Cast not out, I entreat Thee, O my Lord, them that have sought Thee, and turn not away such as have directed their steps towards Thee, and deprive not of Thy grace all that love Thee. Thou art He, O my Lord, Who hath called Himself the God of Mercy, the Most Compassionate. Have mercy, then, upon Thy handmaiden who hath sought Thy shelter, and set her face towards Thee.

Thou art, verily, the Ever-Forgiving, the Most Merciful.[9]

O my God! O my God! Verily, these servants are turning to Thee, supplicating Thy kingdom of mercy. Verily, they are attracted by Thy holiness and set aglow with the fire of Thy love, seeking confirmation from Thy wondrous kingdom, and hoping for attainment in Thy heavenly realm. Verily, they long for the descent of Thy bestowal, desiring illumination from the Sun of Reality. O Lord! Make them radiant lamps, merciful signs, fruitful trees and shining stars. May they come forth in Thy service and be connected with Thee by the bonds and ties of Thy love, longing for the lights of Thy favor. O Lord! Make them signs of guidance, standards of Thine immortal kingdom, waves of the sea of Thy mercy, mirrors of the light of Thy majesty.

Verily, Thou art the Generous. Verily, Thou art the Merciful. Verily, Thou art the Precious, the Beloved.[10]

11

Celebrating Our Diversity

The diversity in the human family should be the
cause of love and harmony, as it is in music
where many different notes blend together
in the making of a perfect chord.
—'ABDU'L-BAHÁ

You often see it on bumper stickers today, or as a motto for a cultural festival at a nearby community center: "Celebrate Diversity." It has become a catchphrase that is being used more and more these days to emphasize that our differences are positive, not negative. For the first time in history, people are beginning to see diversity not as a dividing point or a point of contention, but as something to celebrate and admire. Communities, schools, and businesses are making great efforts to diversify their neighborhoods, populations, and workforces, and families with diverse backgrounds are no longer such a rarity. We realize, as our world grows closer and closer and boundaries are broken down, that the diversity in humanity is an asset and not a stumbling block. Yet do we really understand what diversity is? Are we able to move beyond merely tolerating diversity or observing it from a safe distance to truly embracing and celebrating it? This chapter looks at some of the challenges involved in developing a healthy attitude toward diversity and explores some of the advantages that diversity will bring.

It has long been the dream of people to live in a community where there is no hatred or discrimination, where there are no iniquities committed against people whose only crime is being different. Toward this end many attempts have been made to legislate and enforce laws to make us accountable for hate crimes and acts of bigotry. These have had limited success because, while they may penalize perpetrators for wrongdoing, they cannot change hearts. The heart is where the problem has to be addressed, because that is where the hatred and discrimination are implanted and cultivated, not on the streets where the resulting violence flares and rages. By the time hatred manifests itself in violence, it is difficult to stop. We are often so blinded by the fire that we are unable to see the cause of the flames. Our efforts to overcome hatred need to be redirected.

Above all other unions is that between human beings, especially when it cometh to pass in the love of God. Thus is the primal oneness made to appear; thus is laid the foundation of love in the spirit.[1]

For the same reason that we aim a fire extinguisher at the base of the fire, discovering the root cause of hatred is essential to eliminating it. Contrary to what most of us may believe, fire extinguishers don't put out fires; they put out the cause of the fire. When the cause is gone, the fire goes out by itself. It is the same for hatred and discrimination: We need to find a way of eliminating prejudice at its root. However, this cannot happen until we understand that the cause of the problem isn't necessarily a result of differences in culture, nationality, gender, race, sexual orientation, ethnic background, or any other manifestation of diversity and variety in the human family. The problem is prejudice itself—the human tendency to make judgments without evidence and form opinions based on the assumption that one group of people is somehow superior to another, that one person is inherently better than another. This is the cause of the fire.

As difference in degree of capacity exists among human souls, as difference in capability is found, therefore, individualities will differ one from another. But in reality this is a reason for unity and not for discord and enmity. If the flowers of a garden were all of one color, the effect would be monotonous to the eye; but if the colors are variegated, it is most pleasing and wonderful. The difference in adornment of color and capacity of reflection among the flowers gives the garden its beauty and charm. Therefore, although we are of different individualities, different in ideas and of various fragrances, let us strive like flowers of the same divine garden to live together in harmony. Even though each soul has its own individual perfume and color, all are reflecting the same light, all contributing fragrance to the same breeze which blows through the garden, all continuing to grow in complete harmony and accord.[2]

We have to identify and eliminate our internal individual prejudices before we can truly begin to appreciate our diversity. The first step is not unlike the first step of any twelve-step program of self-improvement or change: We need to admit that we harbor prejudices. As babies, we were born without these biases, but it is almost impossible not to acquire them as we grow up in a world that is riddled with them. America is saturated with prejudice. All of us have to work to purge prejudice from our hearts. When facing our own prejudices, asking God for forgiveness and assistance in overcoming them will help. It may also be helpful to ask for the capacity to forgive ourselves, for guilt and the fear of it can easily perpetuate a problem if we tend to avoid facing things that engender such feelings. Transformation from one state to another, from having prejudice to being free of it, is an act of volition. Perhaps the best choice we can make is to become people who are sincerely confronting our internal prejudices rather than people who remain unaccountable to themselves and to the effect that they have on others.

If we live in a social environment that has established traditional boundaries between peoples defined as "us" and "them," then we are unlikely to appreciate diversity, because we do not see it. Today that segregated society can only be maintained by the denial of individuality and the refusal to consider our shared commonality. Unfortunately, this allows us to decide not only who we think someone else is, but to determine how we are going to treat the other person. We make the mistake of defining who another person is according to certain features of their outward appearance, speech, or behavior. In a segregated society this need not be determined by direct observation, but by merely listening and repeating the pejorative folklore and self-aggrandizing myths circulated by its members. The result is not only a fixed idea but a fixed response. It is a prepackaged visceral reaction that requires no further information and is signalized by sentiments like: "We know all we need to know" and "No matter what happens, we are not going to change our minds." There is a simple reason for such attitudes and responses: We are afraid of the unknown.

Some of us have a deep-seated fear of not knowing what to do or how to respond. We equate this feeling with ignorance, and nobody likes to feel ignorant. We forget, however, that when we encounter others who are different from ourselves, not knowing what to do is exactly the problem the others are having with us. Diversity is a mutual phenomenon. People are not just different from us; people are different from each other.

Consider the world of created beings, how varied and diverse they are in species, yet with one sole origin. All the differences that appear are those of outward form and colour. . . .

So it is with humanity. It is made up of many races, and its peoples are of different colour, white, black, yellow, brown and red—but they all come from the same God, and all are servants to Him. . . .

Let us look . . . at the beauty of diversity, the beauty of harmony.[3]

We may be accustomed to looking at others, but if we stand in the other person's shoes for a moment, it may be easier to understand how we ourselves are being seen. Putting ourselves in that situation is the next obstacle. People sometimes disagree with something or oppose it simply because understanding breaks down barriers, and the fear is that we will become the "other." If we pause to examine this fear, it is quite illogical. Understanding something doesn't mean we have to agree with it or become it. Understanding means that we break down barriers so we can appreciate and become acquainted with the varied approaches to life that exist within the human family.

Consider the flowers of a garden: though differing in kind, color, form and shape, yet, inasmuch as they are refreshed by the waters of one spring, revived by the breath of one wind, invigorated by the rays of one sun, this diversity increaseth their charm, and addeth unto their beauty. Thus when that unifying force, the penetrating influence of the Word of God, taketh effect, the difference of customs, manners, habits, ideas, opinions and dispositions embellisheth the world of humanity. This diversity, this difference is like the naturally created dissimilarity and variety of the limbs and organs of the human body, for each one contributeth to the beauty, efficiency and perfection of the whole. When these different limbs and organs come under the influence of man's sovereign soul, and the soul's power pervadeth the limbs and members, veins and arteries of the body, then difference reinforceth harmony, diversity strengtheneth love, and multiplicity is the greatest factor for coordination.[4]

All religions teach that each of us has our own row to hoe and furrow to plow. These invariably become crooked when we take our eyes off of what we are doing and spend too much time checking to see how straight other people's rows are. Each of us is responsible for our own spiritual development, and it is not our job to judge the progress of others.

When divers shades of thought, temperament and character, are brought together under the power and influence of one central agency, the beauty and glory of human perfection will be revealed and made mani-

fest. Naught but the celestial potency of the Word of God, which ruleth and transcendeth the realities of all things, is capable of harmonizing the divergent thoughts, sentiments, ideas, and convictions of the children of men. Verily, it is the penetrating power in all things, the mover of souls and the binder and regulator in the world of humanity.[5]

Part of the joy inherent in the celebration of diversity is not simply tolerating differences that may or may not be beneficial to us, but appreciating those differences that make us stronger as a group.

Man should know his own self and recognize that which leadeth unto loftiness or lowliness, glory or abasement, wealth or poverty.[6]

If we are to determine what is beneficial, we need to be able to compare our behavior with a standard that is not of our own making. If we have adopted a code of conduct for ourselves that is merely convenient and self-reassuring, there is no way to test it to see if it is conducive to our spiritual growth, because we cannot weigh a standard against itself. Religion has traditionally set the standards for ethical and moral behavior, but if we are not religiously oriented, then we are apt to compare what we believe is right and proper with what a religion says on the subject. However, we shouldn't weigh God's standards against our own. God's understanding of what is beneficial to us is far greater than our own. This is why God gives humanity commandments, laws, and ordinances. Bahá'í scripture states,

> These are the ordinances of God that have been set down in the Books and Tablets by His Most Exalted Pen. Hold ye fast unto His statutes and commandments, and be not of those who, following their idle fancies and vain imaginings, have clung to the standards fixed by their own selves, and cast behind their backs the standards laid down by God.[7]

When we come across elements of diversity that do not seem to fit with our own sense of propriety, we must not lose sight of what God has envisioned for us. Not all things are good relative to cultural context or locale, and not all things are acceptable just because a lot of other people do them. We are bound to encounter some practices that are not beneficial to spiritual growth, but this is not a reason to hate or avoid the people who engage in them. We need to be able to separate the people from their practices and remember that the grace of God rains down on everyone. In like manner we should love and associate with each other, not hate and avoid each other. We are each progressing at our own rate and will, in the course of time, discover for ourselves what we need to do to grow spiritually. Self-destructive practices are to be avoided, not the people who practice them, because people always have the ability to change what they do.

If we are seeking ways to celebrate each other and who we are, prayer is an invaluable tool in that search. Not only does it give us a means by which to ask for God's aid and assistance as we work to move beyond merely tolerating differences to celebrating diversity, it also gives us a means to appreciate that part of us which is completely unique to each individual: our spiritual nature. Our souls, like our bodies, are extremely varied, unique, and precious. And just as there is rich diversity in the physical appearances of human beings, there is also rich diversity in the way that they connect with God in prayer. Even so, every connection is precious, every connection is effective.

Selected Prayers from Bahá'í Scripture

Glorified art Thou, O Lord my God! I implore Thee by the onrushing winds of Thy grace, and by them Who are the Daysprings of Thy purpose and the Dawning-Places of Thine inspiration, to send down upon me and upon all that have sought Thy face that which beseemeth Thy generosity and bountiful grace, and is worthy of Thy bestowals and favors. Poor and desolate I am, O my Lord! Immerse me in the ocean of Thy wealth; athirst, suffer me to drink from the living waters of Thy loving-kindness.

I beseech Thee, by Thine own Self and by Him Whom Thou hast appointed as the Manifestation of Thine own Being and Thy discriminating Word unto all that are in heaven and on earth, to gather together Thy servants beneath the shade of the Tree of Thy gracious providence. Help them, then, to partake of its fruits, to incline their ears to the rustling of its leaves, and to the sweetness of the voice of the Bird that chanteth upon its branches. Thou art, verily, the Help in Peril, the Inaccessible, the Almighty, the Most Bountiful.[8]

O Thou kind Lord! O Thou Who art generous and merciful! We are the servants of Thy threshold and are gathered beneath the sheltering shadow of Thy divine unity. The sun of Thy mercy is shining upon all, and the clouds of Thy bounty shower upon all. Thy gifts encompass all, Thy loving providence sustains all, Thy protection overshadows all, and the glances of Thy favor are cast upon all. O Lord! Grant Thine infinite bestowals, and let the light of Thy guidance shine. Illumine the eyes, gladden the hearts with abiding joy. Confer a new spirit upon all people and bestow upon them eternal life. Unlock the gates of true understanding and let the light of faith shine resplendent. Gather all people beneath the shadow of Thy bounty and cause them to unite in harmony, so that they may become as rays of one sun, as the waves of one ocean, and as the fruit of one tree. May they drink from the same fountain. May they be refreshed by the same breeze. May they receive illumination from the same source of light. Thou art the Giver, the Merciful, the Omnipotent.[9]

12

Serving the Community and the World

Think ye at all times of rendering some service
to every member of the human race.
—'ABDU'L-BAHÁ

At some point in life it may be natural to consider rendering an important service to others. We may be grateful for our own good fortune and wish to give something back for it, or we may have a cause or issue that has great personal meaning to us, a cause to which we would gladly give our time and energy. We commonly view service as something above and beyond what we would "normally" do. But what if we were to expand that concept and infuse the spirit of service—kindness shown without thought of self-promotion or self-gain—into everything we do? What if we were to take the lessons learned from spiritually transforming ourselves, our family life, and the lives of those around us and apply them to our interactions with each other by serving one another? This chapter discusses the spiritual meaning of service and how it can be a catalyst for bringing a community together.

The social and spiritual needs of the world evolve over time and the social requirements of each age differ because civilization itself evolves and changes, and the needs of humanity shift as we progress. To enable us to continue the advancement of civilization, we have been given commandments that are renewed and expanded from time to time by God's prophets.

From the earliest times, love has always been a bond that unites people. However, the circle of who we need to love has grown. At one time, when the possibilities of communication and travel were very limited, it was sufficient to love one another and to love our neighbors as ourselves because everyone else lived so far away. Later, as our exposure to the world expanded, it was appropriate to love the tribe, the city, and the nation to which we belonged as well. Now we need to love the entire family of humankind. In an age when it is possible to communicate instantaneously with people virtually anywhere in the world, no one is too far away to be loved, and one of the best ways we can show that love is by serving each other.

Man's merit lieth in service and virtue and not in the pageantry of wealth and riches.[1]

Love is not the only commandment God has given us that can expand to meet the needs of a worldwide community. In the past we were given an injunction known to us as the Golden Rule, which admonishes us to do unto others as we would have them do unto us. This helped to define our standard of interaction with each other and established the foundation for behavioral reciprocity. The Bahá'í teachings stress that service to others needs to take center stage as a new Golden Rule, declaring that we should prefer others over ourselves. Service is a bond that brings people together; like love, it does not arise from obligation but from a selfless concern for the well-being of others. Service can be a means of worshiping God.

All effort and exertion put forth by man from the fullness of his heart is worship, if it is prompted by the highest motives and the will to do service to humanity. This is worship: to serve mankind and to minister to the needs of the people. Service is prayer.[2]

Man can receive no greater gift than this, that he rejoice another's heart.[3]

In this age the worship of God is not restricted to prayerfulness and piety. Our intentions and actions can be like a prayer in thought and deed, and work performed in the spirit of service is a legitimate form of worship. No matter what our occupation may be, we can pursue it in an attitude of helpfulness and joy. It is no longer sufficient merely to feel love for one another; we must demonstrate that love by helping others. In a time when we distance ourselves from others and content ourselves with loving one another from afar, or understand the concept of caring for each other but don't put it into action, the best way to unite and transform the world we live in is to turn our lofty ideals into tangible deeds. An old proverb states that God helps those who help themselves. This is still true, but God also helps those who help others.

The very act of striving to serve, however unworthy one may feel, attracts the blessings of God and enables one to become more fitted for the task.[4]

God will assist all those who arise in His service.[5]

When we consider how best to serve others, it is helpful to remember that we rise to the level that we set for ourselves. Whatever service we render ought to be performed to the best of our abilities. It is also important to note that while striving for excellence in all that we do, the sincerest form of service is that which is offered in a spirit of humility. To be useful is gratifying, but our efforts to help others should be free from any desire for self-aggrandizement, recognition, or sense of superiority. Prestige is a notion that is based on social beliefs, not on reality.

For example, modern society holds medical doctors in high esteem because they study healing methods for years, they are paid well, and they deal with important matters of life and death. Oftentimes when your health is in great peril, the skills and knowledge of a doctor are essential to cure your ailment or heal your injury. For these reasons we entrust our health care to them and seek them out when we are sick. Garbage collectors, however, are not nearly so highly regarded. Many view the job of a garbage collector as necessary but undesirable because it deals with our refuse, the items that we don't want to deal with anymore. Every day, however, garbage collectors remove and dispose of tons of potentially dangerous materials, thereby ensuring that thousands of people will not fall ill. Garbage collecting is, in fact, far more proactive than traditional medicine in the prevention of disease. On one hand, the majority of medical doctors are not in the business of prevention because they endeavor to treat us only *after* we have become ill. Garbage collectors, on the other hand, perform their service *before* we get sick by preventing the potential spread of disease. So which profession is worthier of prestige and respect? They could be regarded as equal because both doctor and garbage collector serve the world and in so doing serve each other.

Direct your whole effort toward the happiness of those who are despondent, bestow food upon the hungry, clothe the needy, and glorify the humble.[6]

Let them [all human beings] purify their sight and behold all humankind as leaves and blossoms and fruits of the tree of being. Let them at all times concern themselves with doing a kindly thing for one of their fellows, offering to someone love, consideration, thoughtful help.[7]

Every individual . . . is under the obligation of engaging in some work or profession, for work, especially when performed in the spirit of service, is according to Bahá'u'lláh a form of worship. It has not only a utilitarian purpose, but has a value in itself, because it draws us nearer to God, and enables us to better grasp His purpose for us in this world.[8]

Any work that one pursues in life, not just volunteer work, can be pursued with a spirit of service. Any profession, whether it is seen as prestigious or lowly, is worthy of praise if it exists to serve others. Our intentions, efforts, and achievements are all factors in our service to others. To serve effectively we need to be pure-hearted in our intentions, industrious in our efforts, and humble in our achievements.

Placing too much emphasis on outcomes can be disappointing. It is good to be successful, but often the outcome of a situation is beyond our control. Being overly focused on results and the bottom line may be the driving factors in corporations and capitalism, but they have little to do with true service. If we value only the outcome and not the efforts that are made, then the adage "the ends justify the means" makes logical sense. However, experience has repeatedly demonstrated that those of us who follow this rationale are ultimately judged both by the selfishness of our hearts and by what our hands have wrought. Our intentions are the one thing in life over which we have complete control, especially when we endeavor to help each other. They are part of a sequence of steps leading to effective service.

The first step in any plan for effective service should be to begin with prayer, for it is always spiritually beneficial to pray and reflect upon the needs of the situation in which we hope to serve. This helps us to remain selfless in our intentions. Next we must draw upon our resolve and volition, and finally we must act to carry out our plan, confident that whatever the result may be, it is the will of God.

It is incumbent upon every man of insight and understanding to strive to translate that which hath been written into reality and action. . . . That one indeed is a man who, today, dedicateth himself to the service of the entire human race. The Great Being saith: Blessed and happy is he that ariseth to promote the best interests of the peoples and kindreds of the earth.[9]

As a framework for our intentions and an outline for our service to others, the following excerpt from Bahá'í scripture is among the best spiritual advice ever given:

Be generous in prosperity, and thankful in adversity. Be worthy of the trust of thy neighbor, and look upon him with a bright and friendly face. Be a treasure to the poor, an admonisher to the rich, an answerer of the cry of the needy, a preserver of the sanctity of thy pledge. Be fair in thy judgment, and guarded in thy speech. Be unjust to no man, and show all meekness to all men. Be as a lamp unto them that walk in darkness, a joy to the sorrowful, a sea for the thirsty, a haven for the distressed, an upholder and defender of the victim of oppression. Let integrity and uprightness distinguish all thine acts. Be a home for the stranger, a balm to the suffering, a tower of strength for the fugitive. Be eyes to the blind, and a guiding light unto the feet of the erring. Be an ornament to the countenance of truth, a crown to the brow of fidelity, a pillar of the temple of righteousness, a breath of life to the body of mankind, an ensign of the hosts of justice, a luminary above the horizon of virtue, a dew to the soil of the human heart, an ark on the ocean of knowledge, a sun in the heaven of bounty, a gem on the diadem of wisdom, a shining light in the firmament of thy generation, a fruit upon the tree of humility.[10]

Direct, true, and succinct spiritual advice need not always be framed in the form of a commandment beginning with the words: "Thou shalt not . . ." We are all too often confronted with laws defining what we are not allowed to do rather than with spiritual guidance counseling us as to what we should do. Spiritual advice is far more useful as a guide to life than any criminal code. Civil laws are written in an attempt to deter crime and control bad behavior. They are not much different from the rules we often create to control children. Spiritual advice is different because it is given to adults who know that they are responsible for their own compliance. Advice is given without attaching negative sanctions delineating the punishment of failure to comply. Built in to such advice is the recognition that certain things have natural consequences.

The physical universe is governed by laws of nature, and there are natural, inevitable consequences for ignoring things like gravity and inertia. The result of ignoring these natural laws can be painful and injurious to our bodies. Gravity and inertia are always with us, and whenever we attempt to break these laws, whether knowingly or unknowingly, the consequences are, in a sense, self-imposed. There is no need to make a law that states, "Thou shalt not step off the roofs of tall buildings." It is sufficient to advise against it and to explain how natural laws work.

It is the same in the spiritual universe. It should not surprise us to know that there are also spiritual laws at work in the world. There are natural spiritual consequences for running counter to spiritual verities. The spiritual laws are always with us; if we violate them, whether wittingly or unwittingly, the consequences are inevitable and are, in a sense, self-initiated and self-imposed. For example, if we do not endeavor to share what we have or do not strive to address the needs of others, the resulting dynamics of selfishness and indifference are painful to our souls and injurious to our personal spiritual development. However, whenever we comply with the spiritual laws and heed the spiritual advice that is available to us, the rewards are limitless.

Make me ready, in all circumstances, O my Lord, to serve Thee and to set myself towards the adored sanctuary of Thy Revelation and of Thy Beauty. If it be Thy pleasure, make me to grow as a tender herb in the meadows of Thy grace, that the gentle winds of Thy will may stir me up and bend me into conformity with Thy pleasure, in such wise that my movement and my stillness may be wholly directed by Thee.[11]

Assist the world of humanity as much as possible. Be the source of consolation to every sad one, assist every weak one, be helpful to every indigent one, care for ev-

ery sick one, be the cause of glorification to every lowly one, and shelter those who are overshadowed by fear.

In brief, let each one of you be as a lamp shining forth with the light of the virtues of the world of humanity. Be trustworthy, sincere, affectionate and replete with chastity. Be illumined, be spiritual, be divine, be glorious, be quickened of God.[12]

Turning to God in prayer is an appropriate first step if we desire to be of service to others, for God is the source of a strength greater than our own and will guide us to where we can be most useful. After all, service is a sacred activity, and work done in that spirit is akin to a prayer to God.

Selected Prayers from Bahá'í Scripture

O God, and the God of all Names, and Maker of the heavens! I entreat Thee by Thy Name through which He Who is the Dayspring of Thy might and the Dawning-Place of Thy power hath been manifested, through which every solid thing hath been made to flow, and every dead corpse hath been quickened, and every moving spirit confirmed— I entreat Thee to enable me to rid myself of all attachment to any one but Thee, and to serve Thy Cause, and to wish what Thou didst wish through the power of Thy sovereignty, and to perform what is the good pleasure of Thy will.

I beseech Thee, moreover, O my God, to ordain for me what will make me rich enough to dispense with any one save Thee. Thou seest me, O my God, with my face turned towards Thee, and my hands clinging to the cord of Thy grace. Send down upon me Thy mercy, and write down for me what Thou hast written down for Thy chosen ones. Powerful art Thou to do what pleaseth Thee. No God is there but Thee, the Ever-Forgiving, the All-Bountiful.[13]

O God! O God! This is a broken-winged bird and his flight is very slow—assist him so that he may fly toward the apex of prosperity and salvation, wing his way with the utmost joy and happiness throughout the illimitable space, raise his melody in Thy Supreme Name in all the regions, exhilarate the ears with this call, and brighten the eyes by beholding the signs of guidance.

O Lord! I am single, alone and lowly. For me there is no support save Thee, no helper except Thee and no sustainer beside Thee. Confirm me in Thy service, assist me with the cohorts of Thine angels, make me victorious in the promotion of Thy Word and suffer me to speak out Thy wisdom amongst Thy creatures. Verily, Thou art the helper of the weak and the defender of the little ones, and verily Thou art the Powerful, the Mighty and the Unconstrained.[14]

O my God! O my God! Verily, these servants are turning to Thee, supplicating Thy kingdom of mercy. Verily, they are attracted by Thy holiness and set aglow with the fire of Thy love, seeking confirmation from Thy wondrous kingdom, and hoping for attainment in Thy heavenly realm. Verily, they long for the descent of Thy bestowal, desiring illumination from the Sun of Reality. O Lord! Make them radiant lamps, merciful signs, fruitful trees and shining stars. May they come forth in Thy service and be connected with Thee by the bonds and ties of Thy love, longing for the lights of Thy favor. O Lord! Make them signs of guidance, standards of Thine immortal kingdom, waves of the sea of Thy mercy, mirrors of the light of Thy majesty.

Verily, Thou art the Generous. Verily, Thou art the Merciful. Verily, Thou art the Precious, the Beloved.[15]

Afterword

Each of us brings a variety of things home in the course of our lifetime, both to the house in which we dwell and the home within our heart. We are, by nature, collectors of mementos, keepers of the souvenirs of our life experiences. Some of the things we bring home are just curios and novelties, items we once found interesting, but now perhaps less so. Many of them are just ornamental knickknacks and bric-a-brac, the inconsequential little odds and ends that accumulate over a lifetime. We bring them home where they are displayed for a while, but we have no great attachment to them. We know that they are destined to be disposed of or replaced by more meaningful treasures and keepsakes that have special associations attached to them. The kinds of things we value the most tend to have one thing in common: For one reason or another they have become sacred to us. We hold them in reverence because of their deeper significance. These are symbolic and mnemonic in much the same way as a photograph reminds us of the smile of a loved one, an old, tucked-away letter is the repository of our sweetheart's affection, or our child's crayon masterpiece helps us remember that we are forgiven if we sometimes draw outside the lines. Of the many things we bring home, the most sacred to us are the proofs that we are loved.

However, from time to time we get tired of the accumulation of clutter and need to do some major housecleaning. We look at our belongings and dispose of certain things, not just because our home is getting crowded, but because we no longer need all of the things we are keeping. As we clean we take stock of what we have. We invariably come across some of the things we inherited from our parents. Some of these aren't pretty, but because they are part of our heritage, we hesitate to get rid of them. We tell ourselves that we have not yet had enough time to determine their true worth. There are piles of gifts we need to look through, a combination of things we have received from others and things we have given to ourselves. We say to ourselves that the things that still give us solace will stay, and those that don't will go. However, the more we look, the more we find. There are gifts everywhere, whole rooms filled with gifts we had forgotten we received. Unlike the rest of our belongings, gifts are rarely discarded. Regardless of their size or sophistication, they are all cherished because they are the tokens of love. In among the rest are the mysterious gifts that just showed up on our doorstep every so often. These are what we were really hoping to find in our housecleaning. These are the most cherished and sacred things we have because they are the gifts from God, the evidences of His love for us.

After a good cleaning, our home seems much brighter, illumined by the light of all the love we have found. Now, as we pass through the rooms of our home, we can look around and see that we are surrounded by the evidences of our own spirituality. Even in the shadowy corners, we can see signs of mercy and forgiveness. There is a room where the walls are decorated with our own image. Old pictures hang side by side with newer ones—some of them attractive, others less so. They are there to remind us of how much we have progressed and transformed ourselves spiritually. As we stand before them we are proud to see how far we have come, yet we are humbled by how far there is to go.

When we are done housecleaning we can see that it is better than before. As we put things back we arrange them differently than before, changing things around. This is one of the reasons we clean our home from time to time. When our understanding of things changes, our beliefs and views change, too. Many of the things we have are moved many times before we find just the right spot for them. In taking stock we are relieved to find empty spaces here and there throughout the home. These are the places where prejudices and hatred once lurked, and it is good to see some of them gone. We notice that there are still a few of them to be gotten rid of, but maybe next time we take stock more will be missing. We are patient because progress, not perfection, is the goal of housecleaning. In the end we straighten the sign by the front door that reads,

O Son of Being! Thy heart is My home; sanctify it for My descent. Thy spirit is My place of revelation; cleanse it for My manifestation.[1]

Notes

Introduction

1. 'Abdu'l-Bahá, quoted in Shoghi Effendi, *World Order of Bahá'u'lláh*, p. 42.

2. E. G. Browne, quoted in Hasan Balyuzi, *Edward Granville Browne and the Bahá'í Faith*, p. 56.

3. Bahá'u'lláh, quoted in Hasan Balyuzi, *Edward Granville Browne and the Bahá'í Faith*, p. 57.

Part 1 / Turning to God

Chapter 1 / Bringing God into Our Lives

1. Bahá'u'lláh, quoted in Shoghi Effendi, *Advent of Divine Justice*, p. 76.

2. Bahá'u'lláh, *Gleanings from the Writings of Bahá'u'lláh*, pp. 234–35.

3. 'Abdu'l-Bahá, *Selections from the Writings of 'Abdu'l-Bahá*, no. 22:1.

4. 'Abdu'l-Bahá, in *Spiritual Foundations*, no. 25.

5. 'Abdu'l-Bahá, quoted in J. E. Esslemont, *Bahá'u'lláh and the New Era*, p. 93.

6. 'Abdu'l-Bahá, *Promulgation of Universal Peace*, p. 148.

7. 'Abdu'l-Bahá in *Spiritual Foundations*, no. 24.

8. 'Abdu'l-Bahá, *Selections from the Writings of 'Abdu'l-Bahá*, no. 150:3.

9. 'Abdu'l-Bahá, *Paris Talks*, no 1:1.

10. 'Abdu'l-Bahá, *Some Answered Questions*, p. 300.

11. Bahá'u'lláh, *Hidden Words*, Persian, no. 49.

12. 'Abdu'l-Bahá, *Paris Talks*, no. 20:15.

13. 'Abdu'l-Bahá, *Paris Talks*, no. 3:2.

14. 'Abdu'l-Bahá, *Some Answered Questions*, p. 301.

15. Bahá'u'lláh, in *Bahá'í Prayers*, pp. 124–25.

16. Bahá'u'lláh, in *Bahá'í Prayers*, p. 4.

17. 'Abdu'l-Bahá, in *Bahá'í Prayers*, pp. 153–54.

Chapter 2 / Using the Power of Prayer

1. Bahá'u'lláh, *Kitáb-i-Íqán*, p. 194.

2. 'Abdu'l-Bahá, *Selections from the Writings of 'Abdu'l-Bahá*, no. 172:1.

3. 'Abdu'l-Bahá, in *Spiritual Foundations*, no. 25.

4. 'Abdu'l-Bahá, quoted in J. E. Esslemont, *Bahá'u'lláh and the New Era*, p. 94.

5. Shoghi Effendi, in *Bahá'í News*, no. 102 (Aug. 1936), p. 3.

6. Bahá'u'lláh, *Gleanings*, p. 295.

7. Bahá'u'lláh, *Hidden Words*, Persian, no. 5.

8. 'Abdu'l-Bahá, quoted in J. E. Esslemont, *Bahá'u'lláh and the New Era*, p. 94.

9. The Báb, *Selections from the Writings of the Báb*, p. 78.

10. 'Abdu'l-Bahá, *Spiritual Foundations*, no. 22.

11. 'Abdu'l-Bahá, *Paris Talks*, no. 54:11.

12. Extract from a letter dated 26 October 1938 written on behalf of Shoghi Effendi to an individual, in *Compilation of Compilations*, vol. 2, p. 240, no. 1768.

13. The Báb, in *Bahá'í Prayers*, pp. 56–57.

14. 'Abdu'l-Bahá, in *Bahá'í Prayers*, pp. 70–71.

15. 'Abdu'l-Bahá, in *Bahá'í Prayers*, pp. 57–58.

Chapter 3 / Growing Spiritually

1. Bahá'u'lláh, *Gleanings*, p. 299.

2. 'Abdu'l-Bahá, *Paris Talks*, no. 28:6.

3. 'Abdu'l-Bahá, *Paris Talks*, no. 40:35.

4. 'Abdu'l-Bahá, *Selections from the Writings of 'Abdu'l-Bahá*, no. 12:1.

5. 'Abdu'l-Bahá, *Secret of Divine Civilization*, pp. 33–34.

6. 'Abdu'l-Bahá, *Promulgation of Universal Peace*, p. 60.

7. 'Abdu'l-Bahá, *Promulgation of Universal Peace*, p. 142.

8. Bahá'u'lláh, *Hidden Words*, Arabic, no. 5.

9. 'Abdu'l-Bahá, *Selections from the Writings of 'Abdu'l-Bahá*, no. 174:3.

10. 'Abdu'l-Bahá, *Paris Talks*, no. 53:13.

11. Bahá'u'lláh, *Hidden Words*, Persian, no. 9.

12. Bahá'u'lláh, in *Bahá'í Prayers*, pp. 141–42.

13. Bahá'u'lláh, in *Bahá'í Prayers*, pp. 142–43.

14. 'Abdu'l-Bahá, in *Bahá'í Prayers*, p. 37.

Chapter 4 / Dealing with Life's Tests

1. 'Abdu'l-Bahá, *Paris Talks*, no. 14:9.

2. 'Abdu'l-Bahá, *Paris Talks*, no. 57:1.

3. Bahá'u'lláh, *Gleanings*, p. 106.

4. Letter dated 24 February 1923 written on behalf of Shoghi Effendi to an individual, in *Unfolding Destiny*, p. 15.

5. Bahá'u'lláh, *Hidden Words*, Arabic, no. 52.

6. Bahá'u'lláh, *Gleanings*, p. 329.

7. 'Abdu'l-Bahá, *Selections from the Writings of 'Abdu'l-Bahá*, no. 197:1.

8. Shoghi Effendi, *Directives from the Guardian*, p. 71, no. 118.

9. 'Abdu'l-Bahá, *Paris Talks*, no. 28:19.

10. Bahá'u'lláh, in *Consultation: A Compilation*, p. 1, no. 2.

11. 'Abdu'l-Bahá, *Promulgation of Universal Peace*, p. 453.

12. Bahá'u'lláh, *Kitáb-i-Íqán*, p. 8.

13. 'Abdu'l-Bahá, *Selections from the Writings of 'Abdu'l-Bahá*, no. 196:1.

14. 'Abdu'l-Bahá, *Paris Talks*, no. 14:8.

15. The Báb, in *Bahá'í Prayers*, p. 28.

16. 'Abdu'l-Bahá, in *Bahá'í Prayers*, p. 152.

17. Bahá'u'lláh, in *Bahá'í Prayers*, p. 87.

18. Bahá'u'lláh, *Gleanings*, p. 285.

19. Bahá'u'lláh, quoted in Shoghi Effendi, *Advent of Divine Justice*, p. 82.

20. 'Abdu'l-Bahá, *Paris Talks,* no. 35:3.

21. Bahá'u'lláh, in *Bahá'í Prayers,* pp. 26–27.

22. The Báb, in *Bahá'í Prayers,* p. 29.

23. The Báb, in *Bahá'í Prayers,* p. 29.

24. 'Abdu'l-Bahá, in *Bahá'í Prayers,* pp. 32–33.

Part 2 / Nurturing the Family

1. 'Abdu'l-Bahá, in *Compilation of Compilations,* vol. 1, p. 391, no. 839.

Chapter 5 / Building Family Unity

1. 'Abdu'l-Bahá, *Promulgation of Universal Peace,* p. 348.

2. 'Abdu'l-Bahá, *Promulgation of Universal Peace,* p. 168.

3. 'Abdu'l-Bahá, *Promulgation of Universal Peace,* pp. 144–45.

4. 'Abdu'l-Bahá, *Promulgation of Universal Peace,* p. 230.

5. 'Abdu'l-Bahá, *Promulgation of Universal Peace,* p. 9.

6. 'Abdu'l-Bahá, in *Compilation of Compilations,* vol. 1, p. 392, no. 845.

7. 'Abdu'l-Bahá, *Promulgation of Universal Peace,* p. 8.

8. 'Abdu'l-Bahá, *Paris Talks,* no. 9:21.

9. 'Abdu'l-Bahá, in *Compilation of Compilations,* vol. 1, p. 397, no. 859.

10. 'Abdu'l-Bahá, in *Compilation of Compilations,* vol. 1, p. 392, no. 842.

11. 'Abdu'l-Bahá, *Promulgation of Universal Peace,* p. 168.

12. Bahá'u'lláh, in *Bahá'í Prayers,* p. iii.

13. 'Abdu'l-Bahá, in *Bahá'í Prayers,* p. 65.

Chapter 6 / Ensuring Marital Harmony

1. Bahá'u'lláh, in *Bahá'í Prayers,* p. 105.

2. Bahá'u'lláh, in *Compilation of Compilations,* vol. 1, p. 235, no. 526.

3. 'Abdu'l-Bahá, *Selections from the Writings of 'Abdu'l-Bahá,* nos. 92:1–3.

4. 'Abdu'l-Bahá, in *Compilation of Compilations,* vol. 1, p. 397, no. 860.

5. Letter dated 15 April 1939 written on behalf of Shoghi Effendi, *Compilation of Compilations,* vol. 2, p. 446, no. 2316.

6. 'Abdu'l-Bahá, *Selections from the Writings of 'Abdu'l-Bahá,* no. 86:1.

7. Bahá'u'lláh, *Gleanings,* p. 288.

8. Bahá'u'lláh, *Kitáb-i-Aqdas,* para. 70.

9. 'Abdu'l-Bahá, *Paris Talks,* no. 9:5.

10. 'Abdu'l-Bahá, in *Bahá'í Prayers,* p. 106.

11. 'Abdu'l-Bahá, *Selections from the Writings of 'Abdu'l-Bahá,* no. 88:1.

12. 'Abdu'l-Bahá, in *Bahá'í Prayers,* p. 107.

13. 'Abdu'l-Bahá, in *Bahá'í Prayers,* pp. 107–08.

Chapter 7 / Raising Children Spiritually

1. The Universal House of Justice, letter dated Riḍván 2000 to the Bahá'ís of the world, p. 9.

2. 'Abdu'l-Bahá, *Selections from the Writings of 'Abdu'l-Bahá,* no. 99:1.

3. Bahá'u'lláh, in *Compilation of Compilations,* vol. 1, p. 248, no. 565.

4. 'Abdu'l-Bahá, *Selections from the Writings of 'Abdu'l-Bahá,* no. 95:2.

5. The Universal House of Justice, letter dated Riḍván 2000 to the Bahá'ís of the world, p. 9.

6. 'Abdu'l-Bahá, *Promulgation of Universal Peace,* p. 404.

7. 'Abdu'l-Bahá, *Selections from the Writings of 'Abdu'l-Bahá,* no. 102:3.

8. 'Abdu'l-Bahá, *Selections from the Writings of 'Abdu'l-Bahá,* no. 101:1.

9. 'Abdu'l-Bahá, in *Compilation of Compilations,* vol. 1, p. 288, no. 639.

10. 'Abdu'l-Bahá, *Selections from the Writings of 'Abdu'l-Bahá,* no. 114:1.

11. 'Abdu'l-Bahá, *Selections from the Writings of 'Abdu'l-Bahá,* no. 98:2.

12. 'Abdu'l-Bahá, in *Compilation of Compilations,* vol. 1, p. 268, no. 601.

13. 'Abdu'l-Bahá, in *Bahá'í Prayers,* p. 36.

14. Shoghi Effendi, *Bahá'í Administration,* p. 87.

15. 'Abdu'l-Bahá, *Selections from the Writings of 'Abdu'l-Bahá,* no. 103:1.

16. Bahá'u'lláh, *Prayers and Meditations,* pp. 177–78.

17. 'Abdu'l-Bahá, in *Bahá'í Prayers and Tablets for the Young,* p. 25.

18. 'Abdu'l-Bahá, in *Bahá'í Prayers,* p. 37.

19. 'Abdu'l-Bahá, in *Bahá'í Prayers,* pp. 35–36.

20. 'Abdu'l-Bahá, in *Bahá'í Prayers and Tablets for the Young,* p. 10.

Part 3 / Expanding the Circle of Unity

Chapter 8 / Uniting with Each Other and the World

1. Bahá'u'lláh, *Gleanings,* p. 250.

2. Bahá'u'lláh, *Tablets of Bahá'u'lláh,* p. 67.

3. Bahá'u'lláh, *Gleanings,* p. 214.

4. 'Abdu'l-Bahá, *Selections from the Writings of 'Abdu'l-Bahá,* no. 206:9.

5. Bahá'u'lláh, *Hidden Words,* Arabic, no. 68.

6. 'Abdu'l-Bahá, *Promulgation of Universal Peace,* p. 297.

7. 'Abdu'l-Bahá, *Selections from the Writings of 'Abdu'l-Bahá,* no. 207:2.

8. 'Abdu'l-Bahá, *Paris Talks,* no. 39:1.

9. Bahá'u'lláh, *Epistle to the Son of the Wolf,* p. 14.

10. Bahá'u'lláh, *Gleanings,* p. 250.

11. 'Abdu'l-Bahá, *Selections from the Writings of 'Abdu'l-Bahá,* no. 35:8.

12. Bahá'u'lláh, *Tablets,* p. 67.

13. 'Abdu'l-Bahá, *Promulgation of Universal Peace,* p. 9.

14. 'Abdu'l-Bahá, *Promulgation of Universal Peace*, p. 154.

15. 'Abdu'l-Bahá, quoted in Shoghi Effendi, *The World Order of Bahá'u'lláh*, p. 42.

16. 'Abdu'l-Bahá, *Selections from the Writings of 'Abdu'l-Bahá*, no. 225:26.

17. 'Abdu'l-Bahá, *Paris Talks*, no. 42:7.

18. 'Abdu'l-Bahá, *Paris Talks*, no. 39:19.

19. 'Abdu'l-Bahá, *Selections from the Writings of 'Abdu'l-Bahá*, no. 41:3.

20. Bahá'u'lláh, *Gleanings*, p. 216.

21. 'Abdu'l-Bahá, *Selections from the Writings of 'Abdu'l-Bahá*, no. 35:11.

22. 'Abdu'l-Bahá, *Promulgation of Universal Peace*, p. 453.

23. Bahá'u'lláh, in *Bahá'í Prayers*, p. 204.

24. 'Abdu'l-Bahá, in *Bahá'í Prayers*, pp. 101–02.

25. 'Abdu'l-Bahá, in *Bahá'í Prayers*, pp. 174–75.

Chapter 9 / Working toward Racial Unity

1. 'Abdu'l-Bahá, *Promulgation of Universal Peace*, p. 46.

2. 'Abdu'l-Bahá, *Selections from the Writings of 'Abdu'l-Bahá*, nos. 225:22–23.

3. 'Abdu'l-Bahá, in *The Power of Unity*, p. 31.

4. 'Abdu'l-Bahá, *Promulgation of Universal Peace*, p. 51.

5. 'Abdu'l-Bahá, *Promulgation of Universal Peace*, p. 57.

6. Bahá'u'lláh, quoted in Shoghi Effendi, *The Advent of Divine Justice*, p. 37.

7. 'Abdu'l-Bahá, quoted in Shoghi Effendi, *The Advent of Divine Justice*, p. 38.

8. 'Abdu'l-Bahá, *Promulgation of Universal Peace*, p. 57.

9. 'Abdu'l-Bahá, *Promulgation of Universal Peace*, p. 44.

10. 'Abdu'l-Bahá, *Promulgation of Universal Peace*, p. 44.

11. 'Abdu'l-Bahá, in *The Power of Unity*, p. 68.

12. The Báb, in *Bahá'í Prayers*, p. 28.

13. 'Abdu'l-Bahá, in *Bahá'í Prayers*, pp. 70–71.

Chapter 10 / Bringing about Gender Equality

1. 'Abdu'l-Bahá, *Paris Talks,* no. 15:7.

2. Bahá'u'lláh, in *Compilation of Compilations,* vol. 2, p. 379, no. 2145.

3. 'Abdu'l-Bahá, *Promulgation of Universal Peace,* p. 135.

4. 'Abdu'l-Bahá, *Selections from the Writings of 'Abdu'l-Bahá,* no. 227:18.

5. 'Abdu'l-Bahá, *Promulgation of Universal Peace,* p. 74.

6. 'Abdu'l-Bahá, *Promulgation of Universal Peace,* p. 175.

7. 'Abdu'l-Bahá, *Promulgation of Universal Peace,* p. 77.

8. 'Abdu'l-Bahá, *Paris Talks,* no. 40:33.

9. Bahá'u'lláh, *Prayers and Meditations,* pp. 147–48.

10. 'Abdu'l-Bahá, in *Bahá'í Prayers,* pp. 112–13.

Chapter 11 / Celebrating Our Diversity

1. 'Abdu'l-Bahá, *Selections from the Writings of 'Abdu'l-Bahá,* no. 87:2.

2. 'Abdu'l-Bahá, *Promulgation of Universal Peace,* p. 24.

3. 'Abdu'l-Bahá, *Paris Talks,* nos. 15:3, 15:5, and 15:6.

4. 'Abdu'l-Bahá, *Selections from the Writings of 'Abdu'l-Bahá,* no. 225:24.

5. 'Abdu'l-Bahá, *Selections from the Writings of 'Abdu'l-Bahá,* no. 225:25.

6. Bahá'u'lláh, *Tablets,* p. 35.

7. Bahá'u'lláh, *Kitáb-i-Aqdas,* para. 17.

8. Bahá'u'lláh, in *Bahá'í Prayers,* pp. 109–10.

9. 'Abdu'l-Bahá, in *Bahá'í Prayers,* pp. 100–01.

Chapter 12 / Serving the Community and the World

1. Bahá'u'lláh, *Tablets,* p. 138.

2. 'Abdu'l-Bahá, *Paris Talks,* no. 55:1.

3. 'Abdu'l-Bahá, *Selections from the Writings of 'Abdu'l-Bahá,* no. 174:6.

4. Letter dated 4 May 1942 written on behalf of Shoghi

Effendi to an individual, in *Compilation of Compilations*, vol. 2, p. 222, no. 1711.

5. Letter dated 23 November 1941 written on behalf of Shoghi Effendi, in *Compilation of Compilations*, vol. 2, p. 222, no. 1710.

6. 'Abdu'l-Bahá, *Promulgation of Universal Peace*, p. 469.

7. 'Abdu'l-Bahá, *Selections from the Writings of 'Abdu'l-Bahá*, no. 1:3.

8. Extract from a letter written on behalf of Shoghi Effendi, quoted in Bahá'u'lláh, *Kitáb-i-Aqdas*, pp. 193–94.

9. Bahá'u'lláh, *Gleanings*, p. 250.

10. Bahá'u'lláh, *Gleanings*, p. 285.

11. Bahá'u'lláh, *Prayers and Meditations*, p. 240.

12. 'Abdu'l-Bahá, *Promulgation of Universal Peace*, p. 453.

13. Bahá'u'lláh, *Prayers and Meditations*, p. 226.

14. 'Abdu'l-Bahá, in *Bahá'í Prayers*, pp. 188–89.

15. 'Abdu'l-Bahá, in *Bahá'í Prayers*, pp. 112–13.

Afterword

1. Bahá'u'lláh, *Hidden Words*, Arabic, no. 59.

Bibliography

Works of Bahá'u'lláh

Epistle to the Son of the Wolf. Translated by Shoghı
Effendi. 1st pocket-size ed. Wilmette, Ill.: Bahá'í
Publishing Trust, 1988.

Gleanings from the Writings of Bahá'u'lláh. Translated by
Shoghi Effendi. 1st pocket-size ed. Wilmette, Ill.:
Bahá'í Publishing Trust, 1983.

The Hidden Words. Translated by Shoghi Effendi.
Wilmette, Ill.: Bahá'í Publishing Trust, 1939.

The Kitáb-i-Aqdas: The Most Holy Book. 1st pocket-size
ed. Wilmette, Ill: Bahá'í Publishing Trust, 1993.

The Kitáb-i-Íqán: The Book of Certitude. 1st pocket-size ed.
Translated by Shoghi Effendi. Wilmette, Ill.: Bahá'í
Publishing Trust, 1983.

Prayers and Meditations. Translated by Shoghi Effendi.
1st pocket-size ed. Wilmette, Ill.: Bahá'í Publishing
Trust, 1987.

Tablets of Bahá'u'lláh revealed after the Kitáb-i-Aqdas.
Compiled by the Research Department of the Universal House of Justice. Translated by Habib Taherzadeh
et al. Wilmette, Ill.: Bahá'í Publishing Trust, 1988.

Works of the Báb

Selections from the Writings of the Báb. Compiled by the
Research Department of the Universal House of
Justice. Translated by Habib Taherzadeh et al. Haifa:
Bahá'í World Centre, 1976.

Works of 'Abdu'l-Bahá

Paris Talks: Addresses Given by 'Abdu'l-Bahá in 1911.
12th ed. London: Bahá'í Publishing Trust, 1995.

*The Promulgation of Universal Peace: Talks Delivered by
'Abdu'l-Bahá during His Visit to the United States and
Canada in 1912.* Compiled by Howard MacNutt. 2d ed.
Wilmette, Ill.: Bahá'í Publishing Trust, 1982.

The Secret of Divine Civilization. 1st pocket-size ed.
Translated by Marzieh Gail and Ali-Kuli Khan.
Wilmette, Ill.: Bahá'í Publishing Trust, 1990.

Selections from the Writings of 'Abdu'l-Bahá. Compiled by
the Research Department of the Universal House of
Justice. Translated by a Committee at the Bahá'í
World Center and by Marzieh Gail. Wilmette, Ill.:
Bahá'í Publishing Trust, 1997.

Some Answered Questions. Compiled and translated by
Laura Clifford Barney. 1st pocket-size ed. Wilmette,
Ill.: Bahá'í Publishing Trust, 1984.

Other Works

The American Bahá'í, 5 June 2000, vol. 31, no. 4.

Bahá'í News, August 1936, no.102.

Bahá'u'lláh and 'Abdu'l-Bahá. *Bahá'í Prayers and Tablets
for the Young.* Wilmette, Ill.: Bahá'í Publishing Trust,
1978.

Bahá'u'lláh, 'Abdu'l-Bahá, and Shoghi Effendi. *Spiritual
Foundations: Prayer, Meditation, and the Devotional
Attitude: Extracts from the Writings of Bahá'u'lláh,
'Abdu'l-Bahá, and Shoghi Effendi.* Compiled by the
Research Department of the Universal House of
Justice. Wilmette, Ill.: Bahá'í Publishing Trust, 1980.

Bahá'u'lláh, 'Abdu'l-Bahá, Shoghi Effendi, and the
Universal House of Justice. *Consultation: A Compila-
tion: Extracts from the Writings and Utterances of
Bahá'u'lláh, 'Abdu'l-Bahá, Shoghi Effendi, and The
Universal House of Justice.* Compiled by the Research
Department of the Universal House of Justice.
Thornhill, Ont.: Bahá'í Community of Canada, 1980.

Bahá'u'lláh, the Báb, 'Abdu'l-Bahá. *Bahá'í Prayers: A
Selection of Prayers Revealed by Bahá'u'lláh, the Báb,
and 'Abdu'l-Bahá.* New ed. Wilmette, Ill: Bahá'í Publishing Trust, 1991.

Bahá'u'lláh, the Báb, 'Abdu'l-Bahá, Shoghi Effendi, and the Universal House of Justice. *The Power of Unity: Beyond Prejudice and Racism.* Compiled by Bonnie J. Taylor et al. Wilmette, Ill.: Bahá'í Publishing Trust, 1986.

The Compilation of Compilations: Prepared by the Universal House of Justice 1963–1990. 2 vols. Australia: Bahá'í Publications Australia, 1991.

Esslemont, J. E. *Bahá'u'lláh and the New Era: An Introduction to the Bahá'í Faith.* 5th rev. ed. Wilmette, Ill.: Bahá'í Publishing Trust, 1980.

Shoghi Effendi. *The Advent of Divine Justice.* 1st pocket-size ed. Wilmette, Ill.: Bahá'í Publishing Trust, 1990.

———. *Bahá'í Administration: Selected Messages 1922–1932.* 7th ed. Wilmette, Ill.: Bahá'í Publishing Trust, 1974.

———. *Directives of the Guardian.* New Delhi: Bahá'í Publishing Trust, n.d.

———. *God Passes By.* New ed. Wilmette, Ill.: Bahá'í Publishing Trust, 1974.

———. *The Unfolding Destiny of the British Bahá'í Community: The Messages from the Guardian of the Bahá'í Faith to the Bahá'ís of the British Isles.* London: Bahá'í Publishing Trust, 1981.

———. *The World Order of Bahá'u'lláh: Selected Letters.* 1st pocket-size ed. Wilmette, Ill.: Bahá'í Publishing Trust, 1991.

Index